WALL PILATES BOOK FOR WOMEN

Sophy Harrington

TABLE OF CONTENT

INTRODUCTION

Welcome to the refreshing realm of Wall Pilates. Within the confines of these pages lies an invitation to explore a distinctive facet of Pilates — an approach that intertwines tradition with innovation, blending the foundation of Pilates with the support and guidance of the wall.

An Entry Point for Beginners

For those stepping into the world of Pilates for the first time, this journey promises a gentle and enlightening initiation. Wall Pilates is a welcoming doorway, offering a nurturing and accessible entry point for beginners. It's a pathway paved with literal and metaphorical support, guiding you through foundational movements and discoveries.

Breaking Down the Wall Barrier

Often a static object in our surroundings, the wall takes on a new persona in Wall Pilates — a steadfast companion in your fitness journey. It's not just a structure but an anchor, providing stability, support, and the opportunity for deeper stretches and controlled movements.

Embracing Simplicity and Accessibility

Here, simplicity reigns supreme. Exercises and movements are designed to be accessible, understanding the hesitations and uncertainties often accompanying starting something new. Each instruction is crafted carefully to bridge the gap between curiosity and confidence.

Nurturing Mind-Body Harmony

Beyond physicality, Wall Pilates is a gateway to mindfulness — a space where the body and mind converge. Through deliberate movements and conscious breathing, practitioners build strength and foster an intimate connection with their bodies, cultivating a serene balance within.

A Roadmap to Growth

As you turn each page, envision this as more than a manual — it's your roadmap to growth. With patience, perseverance, and an open heart, you'll witness the blossoming of your Pilates journey, celebrating milestones as each movement becomes an exploration and an achievement.

Join Us on this Pilates Voyage

Welcome, dear reader, to the voyage of discovery that is Wall Pilates. Embrace the wall, embrace the teachings, and most importantly, embrace the journey that unfolds. Let's start a journey that shapes our bodies and nurtures our souls.

Let's begin.

HOW TO USE THIS BOOK:
A Guide to Your Wall Pilates Journey

Welcome to the "Wall Pilates Workouts for Women," your comprehensive guide to starting and refining your Wall Pilates practice. This book is designed to support you every step of the way, offering a blend of theoretical knowledge, practical exercises, nutrition advice, and motivational strategies. Whether you're entirely new to Pilates or looking to deepen your practice with the unique benefits of wall exercises, this book will be invaluable. Here's how to make the most of it:

STARTING YOUR JOURNEY

- Begin by immersing yourself in the first chapter. It lays the foundational knowledge you need to understand what Wall Pilates is, its benefits, and how it can transform your body and mind. Learn about the guiding principles, the essentials of setting up your practice space, and how to engage your core effectively with the support of a wall.

THEORETICAL FOUNDATION

- All theoretical knowledge is concisely collected in one chapter, making it easy to grasp Wall Pilates without feeling overwhelmed. This section is crucial for understanding the biomechanics and philosophy behind the exercises.

PRACTICAL APPLICATION

- A corresponding Qr coge/video link is provided for every exercise described in the book. These visual aids ensure you're performing each movement correctly, allowing you to mirror the techniques shown for optimal results.

TAILORING YOUR PRACTICE

- If you have specific questions or encounter common challenges, refer to the **"Answering FAQs and Troubleshooting in Wall Pilates"** section. It's there to help you navigate any hurdles and enhance your practice.
- The **"Common Mistakes and How to Correct Them"** section is designed to guide you through typical pitfalls beginners face and provide clear instructions for improving your technique.

NUTRITIONAL SUPPORT

- Understanding that physical exercise and nutrition go hand in hand, the chapter **"Nutrition Advice for Successful Wall Pilates Journey"** offers dietary tips to fuel your body and mind for Pilates.

STAYING MOTIVATED

- Discover strategies to keep your motivation high in the **"Motivation Tips for Thriving in Wall Pilates"** section. Setting goals, celebrating progress, and varying your routine can all contribute to a fulfilling practice.

- **A 31-day planner** is included to help you establish and stick to a consistent practice schedule, ensuring steady progress in your Wall Pilates journey.

FITTING PILATES INTO YOUR SCHEDULE

- For those with a tight schedule, the **"15-Minute Morning Wall Pilates Routines"** and **"15-Minute Evening Wall Pilates Routines"** offer quick, effective workouts to ensure you can still benefit from Pilates practice amidst a busy lifestyle.

ENHANCING YOUR EXPERIENCE

- Finally, the **"Music Playlist for Pilates"** provides a curated selection of tracks to complement your practice, helping you find rhythm and flow in your movements.

SAFETY FIRST

- Safety precautions and adaptations for individual needs are covered extensively, ensuring that your practice is effective and safe.

THE 28-DAY WALL PILATES EXERCISE PLAN

This structured program guides you through daily exercises and routines designed for beginners. Here's what you need to know about this plan:

- **Daily Structure:** Each day is laid out with clear instructions, starting with more straightforward exercises and gradually increasing complexity. This progression is designed to build strength, flexibility, and confidence in using the wall as a Pilates tool.

- **Video Demonstrations:** Every exercise in the 28-day plan has a corresponding video demonstration accessible via a Qr coge and provided link. These videos ensure you have visual guidance to perform each movement correctly, enhancing your understanding and execution of the exercises.

- **Customization Tips:** While the plan is structured, it's also flexible. Adjustments and modifications are provided for different fitness levels and capabilities, ensuring everyone can participate and benefit from the exercises.

BONUSES FOR A HOLISTIC APPROACH

- **Cookbook and Meal Plans:** A bonus cookbook with 65 specially curated recipes and 14 day meal plans supports your physical activities with proper nutrition, ensuring a holistic approach to health. Enhance your Pilates journey with the Cookbook featuring recipes tailored to support your physical efforts with nutritious, balanced meals.

- **Video Library:** Easy-to-navigate, numbered videos for each exercise remove the guesswork from your practice, ensuring you perform each movement precisely. Each video is numbered according to the section and exercise number.

- **Fitness Tracker Downloads:** Accessible for printing, these trackers can be a daily visual reminder, helping you to stay on track with your fitness routine.

This book is more than just a guide; it's a companion on your journey to a healthier, more balanced self through the unique practice of Wall Pilates.

If you have any questions, suggestions, or feedback, please don't hesitate to reach out to us via email **sophy.harrington@proton.me.** We greatly value your input and are always open to hearing from you.

CHAPTER 1. DISCOVERING WALL PILATES

Step into the world of Wall Pilates, where tradition meets innovation, and the wall becomes your ally in pursuing holistic well-being. In this chapter, we explore — unveiling a practice that transcends mere exercise, embracing a lifestyle that nurtures body, mind, and spirit.

The Wall: Your Partner in Transformation

At the heart of Wall Pilates lies a transformative tool — the wall. What may seem like a static structure becomes a dynamic and versatile asset in your journey. It's more than a surface; it's a source of stability, a guide for alignment, and a canvas for creativity in movement.

Breaking Through Conventional Limits

Pilates on the mat is revered for its grace and precision, but Wall Pilates extends beyond these boundaries. It empowers practitioners — especially beginners — with newfound possibilities. The wall serves as an extension of the mat, amplifying the benefits and offering a multifaceted approach to movement.

Embracing Foundations, Expanding Horizons

As beginners, your initiation into Wall Pilates unveils the foundational principles — alignment, control, breath, and flow — that infuse each exercise. But beyond these principles lies a horizon of potential, waiting to be explored and nurtured as your practice evolves.

Harmony in Motion

This isn't just about physical fitness. Wall Pilates cultivates a deeper relationship between body and mind. With each intentional movement, you develop mindfulness, connecting breath with motion and fostering a sense of harmony that transcends the studio's walls.

A Journey of Self-Discovery

Within these chapters, you're not just learning exercises but starting a journey — a discovery of your body's capabilities and nuances. It's an opportunity to tap into your potential, listen to your body, and nurture it through mindful, intentional movement.

The Promise of Wall Pilates

The promise of Wall Pilates is multifaceted — strength, flexibility, balance, and a profound sense of well-being. But beyond these physical attributes, it offers a space for personal growth, resilience, and self-awareness, unveiling layers of your being as you progress.

Defining Wall Pilates: Elevating the Practice

An Evolution in Pilates Practice

Wall Pilates emerges as a beacon of innovation in the vast fitness landscape. It encapsulates the core principles of traditional Pilates while embracing a revolutionary integration — the wall. This alliance transforms the practice, unveiling new dimensions and possibilities.

The Wall: Catalyst for Transformation

Picture the wall not just as a static boundary but as an active participant in your Pilates journey. It becomes a support system, enhancing stability and alignment. The wall's presence offers unique tactile feedback, guiding your body's positioning, refining movements, and amplifying the effectiveness of exercises.

Advantages Beyond the Mat

While traditional mat exercises rely solely on body resistance, Wall Pilates expands the repertoire by incorporating the wall as a support mechanism. This integration transcends limitations, offering advantages such as heightened stability, increased range of motion, and a deeper engagement of muscles.

Wall as a Guide to Stability

Imagine perfecting a posture or movement with the unwavering guidance of the wall. In Wall Pilates, practitioners discover heightened stability — a secure foundation for precise execution. This stability cultivates confidence, especially for beginners, enabling them to explore movements with assurance and ease.

Supporting Alignment: Wall's Tactile Feedback

Alignment is the cornerstone of Pilates, and the wall becomes an ally in this pursuit. Its tactile presence offers instant feedback — assisting in maintaining proper posture and alignment. This feedback loop empowers beginners, facilitating a better understanding of optimal body positioning.

Facilitating Progression: Versatility in Movement

The wall doesn't confine movement; it expands possibilities. It is a versatile tool that adapts to various exercises and allows for incremental progression. As beginners navigate through Wall Pilates, the wall stands ready to support, challenge, and accompany their growth.

A Gateway to Holistic Wellness

Wall Pilates isn't just a workout — it's a gateway to a comprehensive well-being journey. It fosters a mind-body connection, encouraging mindfulness and nurturing a sense of balance and harmony that transcends the confines of a studio.

Unveiling the Pillars of Wall Pilates: Guiding Principles for Beginners

Alignment

Alignment is the cornerstone of Wall Pilates. Picture the wall as your guiding compass, ensuring your body maintains proper positioning and engagement. Each movement becomes an exploration of alignment, allowing beginners to discover the ideal balance between posture and fluidity.

Control

Controlled movements within Wall Pilates offer a canvas for beginners to refine their mastery. Supported by the wall, each exercise invites practitioners to cultivate motion precision. The wall's stability becomes a partner, fostering control as beginners traverse through deliberate and intentional movements.

Breath

Breath becomes the rhythm that harmonizes mind and body. In Wall Pilates, the wall witnesses the cadence of inhalations and exhalations, syncing with movements. As beginners learn to unite breath with motion, a deeper connection to their practice unfolds — a connection rooted in awareness and serenity.

Flow

Imagine movements unfolding seamlessly, like a dance. Wall Pilates encourages beginners to embrace the concept of flow — an artful integration of exercises facilitated by the wall's support. Transitions between poses become graceful, creating an uninterrupted continuum of movement and energy.

Mindful Exploration

Embracing these principles isn't merely about perfecting exercises; it's a mindful exploration — a journey of self-discovery. As beginners venture into Wall Pilates, they uncover the potential of their bodies, nurturing a sense of mindfulness that transcends the studio into everyday life.

An Ongoing Journey of Mastery

The principles of Wall Pilates aren't just teachings; they're pathways to continual growth. Beginners set foot on a journey of embracing alignment, honing control, synchronizing breath, and weaving fluidity, unveiling the potential for mastery and transformation.

Pilates Principles

Principle	Description
Breathing	Pilates emphasizes proper breathing techniques, coordinating breath with movement to increase oxygen flow and control.
Concentration	Focused attention on precise movements helps build a mind-body connection, enhancing the effectiveness of exercises.
Control	Executing movements with control and precision, ensuring muscles are engaged properly while avoiding unnecessary strain.
Centering	Engaging the core or "powerhouse" muscles is pivotal, providing stability and initiating movement from the center outward.
Precision	Performing each movement with accuracy and exactness, aiming for quality over quantity to maximize benefits.
Flow or Fluidity	Smooth, continuous movements encourage grace and efficiency, avoiding jerky or abrupt transitions between exercises.

Importance:

Understanding these principles is vital as they form the foundation of Pilates practice, influencing the effectiveness and safety of exercises. Each principle contributes to enhancing strength, flexibility, and overall body awareness.

THE ESSENTIALS OF WALL PILATES

The Power of Preparation

Begin by envisioning your Wall Pilates sanctuary. Choose a clean, unobstructed wall space, ideally free from distractions. Prepare your environment — ensure the wall is transparent and the floor is conducive to movement. Lay down your mat, providing a comfortable foundation for your practice.

Think of this space as a canvas awaiting your mindful movement and discovery.

Setting Up for Success

The wall becomes your silent companion in this journey. Opt for a smooth, clean surface that allows for movement and comfort during exercises. It's not just a structure; it's your support system, offering stability and guidance. Align yourself facing the wall, allowing adequate space for maneuvering without constraints.

Minimalist Equipment

In the realm of Wall Pilates, simplicity is vital. You only need a dependable yoga or exercise mat — a grounding foundation to cushion your movements and provide stability. Keep it minimal; the focus lies not on the equipment but on the mindful engagement with your body and the wall.

Cultivating Mindful Awareness

Enter the realm of Wall Pilates by acquainting yourself with foundational breathing techniques. Start with diaphragmatic breathing — inhale deeply through the nose, allowing the belly to expand, then exhale through pursed lips, engaging the core. This breathwork establishes a connection between body and mind, fostering focus and control.

Alignment and Intention: Lay the Groundwork

The essence of Wall Pilates rests on alignment and intention. Embrace proper alignment — let the wall guide, ensuring correct posture and engagement. Approach each movement with intention, understanding its purpose and fostering mindful execution.

Beginner's Mind

Approach your Wall Pilates practice with a beginner's mind — a sense of curiosity and openness. This practice isn't just about physical fitness; it's an invitation to explore your body, mind, and breath in unison. Embrace each session as a learning opportunity for growth and self-discovery.

Your Pilates Sanctuary Awaits

These essentials pave the way for your initial steps into Wall Pilates. Imagine your space as a sanctuary where mindful movement meets introspection. Embrace the simplicity, harness the wall's power, and let your breath guide this transformative journey.

Essential Equipment and Setup for Beginners

Equipment	Description	Purpose
Wall Space	A clear, unobstructed wall area, preferably without interruptions like wall hangings or furniture.	Serves as a stable support for various exercises, facilitating balance, stability, and leverage.
Yoga Mat or Towel	Provides a padded surface for exercises, ensuring comfort and preventing slipping.	Cushions body during floor exercises and enhances stability while maintaining grip.
Pilates Ball	A small inflatable ball, around 9-12 inches in diameter.	Adds challenge and variety to exercises, enhances engagement of core and stabilizing muscles.

Equipment	Description	Purpose
Resistance Bands	Elastic bands of varying resistance levels.	Provides additional resistance, improving muscle tone.
Pilates Ring (Magic Circle)	Circular resistance ring made of flexible metal or rubber.	Adds resistance for toning exercises, particularly targeting the inner and outer thighs.
Water Bottle	Hydration is crucial during workouts.	Ensures proper hydration, aiding in optimal performance and recovery.
Comfortable Attire	Form-fitting, breathable clothing allowing free movement.	Ensures comfort, flexibility, and ease of movement during exercises.
Mirror or Full-Length Reflection	Allows visual feedback on posture and form during exercises.	Helps in maintaining proper alignment and ensuring correct execution of movements.

Discovering the Power of Breath: Foundation for Your Pilates Routine

Breath

In Wall Pilates, the breath guides each movement and fosters a connection between body and mind. Begin by acknowledging the significance of breath — it's more than inhaling and exhaling; it's a conduit for mindful awareness and control.

Diaphragmatic Breathing: The Root of Mindful Engagement

Start your journey with diaphragmatic breathing — a foundational technique harmonizing breath and movement. Inhale deeply through your nose, allowing your belly to expand like a balloon filling with air. As you exhale through pursed lips, engage your core, gently drawing the belly button in towards the spine. This breathwork cultivates relaxation, steadies the mind, and fosters a deeper connection to your body's movements.

Coordinating Breath with Movement

As you engage in Wall Pilates exercises, synchronize your breath with deliberate movements. For instance, inhale as you prepare for a movement or stretch, allowing the breath to expand your body, and exhale as you exert effort or contract muscles, guiding them back to a neutral position. This conscious synchronization infuses rhythm and flow into your practice, enhancing control and fluidity.

Mindful Breathing Beyond the Mat: Integrating in Daily Life

Beyond the confines of your Wall Pilates practice, carry the essence of mindful breathing into your everyday life. Embrace moments of conscious breathing — during daily activities, when feeling stressed, or when needing a moment of calm. The breath awareness and control principles extend far beyond the mat, contributing to a more balanced and centered lifestyle.

Breath: Your Ever-Present Companion

Remember, breath is your constant companion throughout your Wall Pilates journey. It's your anchor, guide, and source of inner strength. Embrace the power of breath as you embark on this transformative path — it's not just about movement; it's about nurturing a deeper connection with yourself.

Breathing Techniques

Breathing Technique	Description	Benefits
Diaphragmatic Breathing	Inhale deeply through the nose, expanding the abdomen, then exhale fully, drawing the navel towards the spine. Focus on filling the lower lungs with air.	Enhances oxygenation, reduces stress, improves posture, aids in core activation, and encourages relaxation.
Rib Cage Breathing	Inhale deeply, expanding the rib cage laterally while keeping the abdomen still. Exhale fully, allowing the rib cage to gently contract.	Improves lung capacity, encourages expansion of the rib cage, enhances intercostal muscle engagement, and promotes better thoracic mobility.
Thoracic Breathing	Inhale deeply, focusing on expanding the upper chest and rib cage while keeping the abdomen and lower ribs still. Exhale fully, allowing the chest to relax and contract.	Increases mobility in the upper chest and shoulders, aids in relieving tension, and promotes better oxygen exchange in the upper lungs.
Three-Part Breath	Inhale sequentially into three parts: start with the abdomen, then expand the rib cage, and finally fill the upper chest. Exhale in reverse order: first release the chest, then the rib cage, and finally draw the navel towards the spine.	Enhances full lung capacity, promotes relaxation, encourages awareness of different breathing zones, and aids in core activation.

Pursed Lip Breathing	Inhale slowly through the nose, then exhale gently through pursed lips, as if blowing out a candle. Focus on controlling the exhalation.	Assists in maintaining airway pressure, slows down breathing rate, aids in relaxation, and reduces the feeling of breathlessness.
Counted Breathing	Inhale for a count of four, hold for a count of two, and exhale for a count of six. Adjust counts based on comfort.	Encourages controlled breathing, aids in relaxation, and promotes focus on breath rhythm.

UNDERSTANDING THE BODY–WALL CONNECTION

The Wall as Your Anchor: Stability and Support

In Wall Pilates, the wall isn't merely a boundary; it's an ally — a steadfast source of stability and support. Picture the wall as an extension of your mat, offering a secure foundation for your movements. It becomes a guiding force, aiding in alignment and ensuring proper engagement of muscles during exercises.

Tactile Feedback: Sensing Alignment and Precision

As you engage with the wall, it provides invaluable tactile feedback. Each touchpoint with the wall offers cues for alignment — enabling you to adjust and refine your posture. This feedback loop enhances precision, achieving optimal positioning and fostering a deeper understanding of your body's alignment in various movements.

Supporting Range of Motion: Expanding Possibilities

The wall acts as a boundary that extends your range of motion. It provides a surface against which you can gently press or lean, allowing for deeper stretches and increased flexibility. This support encourages exploration, enabling you to access movements that may have felt inaccessible before.

Creating Resistance: Amplifying Strength

Engaging the wall introduces resistance — a subtle yet effective means of enhancing strength. Utilize the wall's support to push or press against, activating muscles and intensifying the challenge in specific exercises. This resistance contributes to muscle engagement and development, supporting your journey towards increased strength and stability.

Alignment and Posture: The Wall's Silent Instruction

The wall serves as a silent instructor, guiding your alignment and posture. Using it as a reference point, you can check your positioning — ensuring proper spinal alignment, pelvic stability, and muscular engagement. Over time, this consistent alignment practice builds muscle memory, promoting better posture beyond your Pilates practice.

Core Engagement and Stability: The Pillars of Wall Pilates

Core Activation

In Wall Pilates, the core is the focal point — a powerhouse that initiates and supports movements. Visualize it as your body's stabilizing center, comprising not just the abs but also the back, hips, and pelvis. Engaging the core in each movement forms the cornerstone of stability and strength.

The Wall as Stability Support

Utilize the wall as your stability anchor during exercises. As you press or lean against it, engage your core muscles — feel them activate to maintain proper alignment and stability. This interaction with the wall deepens your understanding of how core engagement contributes to balance and control in every movement.

Controlled Movements

Every Wall Pilates movement emphasizes control — a deliberate execution guided by core engagement. Initiate movements from your core — feel the muscles activate before extending or contracting limbs. This conscious control not only refines the movement's precision but also minimizes the risk of strain or injury.

Core-Centric Exercises

Wall Pilates offers a myriad of exercises designed to target core muscles specifically. From leg raises to planks against the wall, each movement challenges and strengthens your core. Embrace these exercises as opportunities to build endurance, stability, and a deeper connection with your body's center.

Core Resilience

Consistent core engagement in Wall Pilates cultivates endurance — which is crucial for sustaining movements. As you progress, notice how your core becomes more resilient, enabling you to maintain stability for longer durations and enhancing your ability to perform exercises with greater ease and control.

The Core's Role

The emphasis on core engagement and stability in Wall Pilates isn't just about physical fitness — it's about nurturing a solid foundation for overall wellness. As you delve deeper into these principles, witness the transformation. This more robust, more stable core supports you in both movement and daily life.

SAFETY AND PRECAUTIONS IN WALL PILATES

Understanding Your Body: Individual Limitations

Wall Pilates beginners should begin their practice by acknowledging their body's unique capacities and limitations. Respect your body's signals — immediately pay attention to any discomfort, pain, or unusual sensations. Listen attentively and honor your body's needs throughout your practice.

The Value of Instruction

Consider seeking guidance from a certified Pilates instructor, especially as a beginner. A qualified instructor ensures proper technique, offers modifications tailored to your abilities, and provides invaluable guidance in navigating exercises safely. Their expertise helps you understand movements, prevent injury, and optimize your practice.

Mindful Progression: Gradual Advancement

Progress in Wall Pilates should be gradual and mindful. Avoid the temptation to rush through exercises or attempt advanced movements prematurely. Start with foundational exercises, gradually increasing intensity or complexity as you gain strength, stability, and confidence.

Warm-Up Ritual

Always consider a proper warm-up. Engage in gentle movements, stretches, and controlled breathing to prepare your body for the exercises. This ritual primes your muscles, enhances flexibility, and reduces the risk of strains or injuries during your practice.

Posture Awareness

Maintaining proper posture throughout exercises is fundamental. Pay attention to alignment cues — keep your spine neutral, engage your core, and ensure balanced weight distribution. Correct posture optimizes exercise effectiveness and minimizes the likelihood of undue stress on muscles or joints.

Breath as a Guide

Sync your breath with movements, using it as a control and body awareness guide. Mindful breathing enhances stability, aids relaxation, and effectively engages the core. Focused breathing ensures a more controlled and conscious practice, reducing the risk of overexertion or strain.

Modifications and Adaptations

Be open to changes and adaptations. Not every exercise will suit your body in the same way. Modify poses as needed to accommodate any physical limitations or discomfort. A skilled instructor can provide variations that align with your abilities while maintaining the exercise's essence.

Rest and Recovery

Acknowledge the importance of rest and recovery in your practice. Allow your body adequate time to recuperate between sessions. Overexertion or inadequate recovery can lead to fatigue or potential injuries. Honor rest as an integral part of your Pilates journey.

Mindful Exit: Listening to Your Body

As crucial as mindfully starting your practice is exiting it with equal attentiveness. After your session, take note of how your body feels. Reflect on any discomfort or areas that need attention, enabling you to adjust your practice in subsequent sessions accordingly.

Community and Support: Seeking Advice

Connect with the Wall Pilates community or seek advice from experienced practitioners. Their shared experiences, insights, and guidance can offer valuable perspectives, tips, and encouragement, fostering a supportive environment for your practice.

Your Pilates Journey: A Safe and Nurturing Path

Safety in Wall Pilates isn't just about avoiding injuries — it's about fostering a nurturing and sustainable practice. By prioritizing safety measures, respecting your body's needs, and seeking professional guidance, your Pilates journey becomes a fulfilling and rewarding exploration of strength, stability, and well-being.

Tailoring Wall Pilates for Individual Needs

Understanding Individual Needs

In Wall Pilates, acknowledging and accommodating diverse physical considerations or limitations is essential. Each individual has unique needs — whether due to injury, flexibility issues, joint concerns, or other physical conditions. Understanding these variations lays the groundwork for personalized modifications.

Customizing Practice

Seeking guidance from a certified Pilates instructor becomes pivotal for individuals with specific considerations. An experienced instructor can offer personalized modifications and variations tailored to individual needs. Their expertise ensures safe and practical exercises, making Wall Pilates accessible and beneficial for a broader range of practitioners.

Joint Mobility

Adjustments in exercises become crucial for those with limited joint mobility. Wall Pilates offers the flexibility to adapt movements — such as reducing the range of motion or modifying angles — to accommodate restricted joint mobility. These modifications ensure engagement without compromising safety or exacerbating discomfort.

Muscle Weakness or Injury

Individuals recovering from muscle weakness or injury require gentle yet effective exercises. Modifications focus on gradual progression and targeted strengthening without straining vulnerable muscles. For instance, using the wall as support during leg raises or incorporating gentle stretches aids in rehabilitation while minimizing risks.

Spinal Issues

Individuals with spinal concerns benefit from modifications that prioritize spinal alignment and support. Exercises can be adapted to maintain a neutral spine or to reduce pressure on the back, allowing engagement without aggravating existing conditions. Techniques that gently engage core muscles while respecting spinal limitations are particularly beneficial.

Balance Challenges

Those facing balance challenges find support and stability through modifications in Wall Pilates. The wall becomes a valuable aid — providing a stable surface against which to lean or support body weight during exercises. These adjustments enhance safety, allowing individuals to focus on controlled movements without compromising balance.

Pregnancy Modifications

Pregnant individuals can benefit from modifications that prioritize safety and comfort. Wall Pilates exercises can be adapted to accommodate changes in body posture and support the changing center of gravity. Emphasizing gentle movements and avoiding prone or supine positions ensure a safe and comfortable practice.

Breath-Centered Modifications: Mind-Body Connection

For individuals with specific health considerations, focusing on breath-centered modifications becomes essential. Emphasizing controlled breath patterns aids relaxation, reduces stress, and fosters a deeper mind-body connection. These modifications prioritize breath as a guide for controlled, mindful movements.

Consistent Adaptations

Modifications in Wall Pilates aren't just temporary adjustments — they're an evolving aspect of practice. As practitioners progress, modifications may change to accommodate improvements or changing physical conditions. Continual adaptation ensures a practice that remains supportive and aligned with individual needs.

Modifications and variations in Wall Pilates empower individuals by making the practice accessible to diverse needs. These adaptations ensure inclusivity, fostering a sense of empowerment and encouraging individuals to engage in a practice that honors their bodies, abilities, and unique circumstances.

ANSWERING FAQS AND TROUBLESHOOTING IN WALL PILATES

1. **What should I wear during Wall Pilates?**
Comfort is key! Opt for form-fitting, breathable attire that allows for ease of movement. Avoid clothes that may restrict movement or become uncomfortable during exercises.

2. **How often should I practice Wall Pilates?**
Consistency matters more than frequency. Initially, aim for 2-3 sessions per week, gradually increasing as you build strength and confidence. Listen to your body and avoid overexertion.

3. **I feel discomfort during specific exercises. What should I do?**
Discomfort isn't uncommon, especially for beginners. However, if you experience pain, stop immediately. Check your posture, alignment, and breathing. Consider modifications or seek guidance from an instructor.

4. **Can Wall Pilates help with back pain?**
Yes! Wall Pilates emphasizes core strength and proper alignment, often alleviating back pain. However, consult a healthcare professional before starting any new exercise routine, especially if dealing with chronic pain.

5. **I'm not flexible. Can I still do Wall Pilates?**
Absolutely! Flexibility isn't a prerequisite. Wall Pilates promotes flexibility gradually. Focus on gentle stretching and

movements, gradually improving flexibility over time.

6. **I need more space at home. Can I still practice Wall Pilates?**
Absolutely! You only need a little space. Adjust exercises to fit your environment. Consider using a door or any available wall space for exercises.

7. **How can I avoid feeling dizzy during specific movements?**
Dizziness can occur if you change positions too quickly. Practice movements slowly and mindfully. Focus on controlled breathing and take breaks if needed.

8. **I need to feel more challenged. What can I do?**
Experiment with variations or gradually increase repetitions. Once you've mastered foundational exercises, explore advanced variations under professional guidance.

9. **Is it normal to feel fatigued after Wall Pilates?**
Yes, especially when starting. Wall Pilates engages various muscles. Fatigue is normal, but listen to your body. Rest and proper hydration are essential for recovery.

10. **How can I progress in Wall Pilates?**
Celebrate small victories! Progress gradually by increasing repetitions, trying new exercises, or mastering advanced variations. Consult an instructor for guidance on advancing safely.

Troubleshooting Tips

- **Feeling Unstable:** Focus on your core engagement and alignment against the wall. Slow down movements and adjust your posture for better stability.

- **Experiencing Pain:** Stop immediately if you feel pain. Check your form, modify the movement, or consult an instructor to avoid injury.
- **Lack of Progress:** Patience is vital. Stay consistent, reassess your goals, and consider seeking guidance for a more tailored approach to your practice.

COMMON MISTAKES AND HOW TO CORRECT THEM

1. **Poor Posture and Alignment**
Mistake: Incorrect posture compromises exercise effectiveness and can lead to strain.
Correction: Focus on alignment — engage the core, keep the spine neutral, and distribute weight evenly. Utilize the wall as a reference for proper alignment. Check your posture frequently during exercises.

2. **Overexertion**
Mistake: Pushing too hard too soon may lead to fatigue, discomfort, or injury.
Correction:
1. Listen to your body.
2. Start with foundational exercises and gradually increase intensity.
3. Take breaks if needed and avoid overexertion.
Quality over quantity is vital.

3. **Holding Your Breath**
Mistake: Holding breath disrupts the flow of movement and reduces oxygen supply to muscles.
Correction: Sync breathing with movements — inhale before the exertion

phase, exhale during the effort — practice controlled breathing to maintain rhythm and ease through exercises.

4. Rushing Movements

Mistake: Rapid, uncontrolled movements compromise form and effectiveness.

Correction: Slow down! Focus on controlled, deliberate movements. Ensure each movement is precise and aligned. Quality movement trumps speed.

5. Neglecting Core Engagement

Mistake: Lack of core engagement diminishes exercise efficacy and stability.

Correction:

1. Prioritize core engagement in every movement.
2. Activate core muscles before initiating any exercise.
3. Visualize pulling the belly button towards the spine to engage your core effectively.

6. Ignoring Modifications

Mistake: Disregarding modifications or variations leads to improper execution or overexertion.

Correction:

1. Embrace modifications tailored to your needs.
2. If an exercise feels uncomfortable, modify it.
3. Seek guidance from an instructor for suitable adaptations.

7. Lack of Warm-Up and Cool-Down

Mistake: Skipping warm-ups or cool-downs increases the risk of injury or post-exercise discomfort.

Correction: Always start with a gentle warm-up to prepare muscles and end with a cool-down to aid recovery. Incorporate stretches and controlled breathing in these routines.

8. Poor Focus on Form

Mistake: Sacrificing form for quantity compromises exercise benefits and increases injury risk.

Correction: Prioritize proper form over the number of repetitions. Concentrate on precise execution, ensuring correct alignment and engagement throughout.

9. Not Listening to Your Body

Mistake: Ignoring signals of discomfort or pain leads to potential injuries.

Correction:

1. Respect your body's cues.
2. If you feel pain or discomfort, stop immediately.
3. Modify the movement or seek guidance from an instructor to avoid injury.

10. Lack of Consistency

Mistake: Inconsistency hampers progress and limits the benefits of practice.

Correction: Establish a consistent practice routine. Regularity is vital to improvement. Aim for a manageable schedule and stick to it.

Correcting these mistakes requires patience, mindfulness, and a commitment to form. Embrace these corrections as opportunities to refine your practice, ensuring a safer, more effective, and transformative experience in Wall Pilates.

NUTRITION ADVICE FOR SUCCESSFUL WALL PILATES JOURNEY

Balanced Meals

Ensure your meals include a balance of macronutrients — proteins, carbohydrates, and healthy fats. Protein aids in muscle repair, carbohydrates provide energy, and healthy fats support overall health. Aim for colorful, nutrient-dense foods to nourish your body and fuel your workouts effectively.

Hydration Matters

Stay hydrated throughout the day, especially before and after workouts. Proper hydration supports bodily functions, aids muscle function, and helps prevent fatigue during exercise. Make it a habit to sip water regularly, and consider electrolyte-rich drinks for intense sessions.

Pre-Workout Nutrition

Consuming a light snack containing carbohydrates and proteins about 30-60 minutes before your workout provides readily available energy. Opt for easily digestible foods like a banana with nut butter or yogurt with fruit to fuel your session without feeling weighed down.

Post-Workout Recovery

Within 30-60 minutes of exercise, aim for a meal rich in carbohydrates and proteins. This aids muscle recovery, replenishes glycogen stores, and supports the repair of muscle tissue. Options like a smoothie with protein powder or a turkey and vegetable wrap are ideal.

Smart Snacking: Nourish Between Meals

Choose nutrient-dense snacks like fruits, nuts, yogurt, or whole-grain crackers to keep energy levels steady between meals. These snacks provide sustained energy, essential vitamins, and minerals without unnecessary calories.

Portion Control and Awareness

Practice portion control and mindful eating. Pay attention to hunger and avoid overeating. Eating slowly and savoring each bite aids digestion, helps maintain a healthy weight.

Minimize Processed Choices

Minimize processed and sugary foods in favor of whole, natural options. Whole foods are rich in nutrients, contain fewer additives, and contribute to overall health and reduced inflammation. Focus on foods that nourish your body and support your active lifestyle.

Variety and Balance

Include a variety of products from different food groups in your meals. A colorful plate signifies a diversity of nutrients. Embrace vegetables, fruits, whole grains, lean proteins, and healthy fats to ensure a well-rounded diet supporting your Pilates practice.

Restorative Sleep

Quality sleep is crucial for recovery. Aim for 7-9 hours of quality sleep each night. Adequate rest supports muscle recovery, enhances mental focus, and contributes to overall well-being, allowing the body to repair and recharge.

Seek Professional Guidance

Consider consulting a registered nutritionist for personalized guidance. They can offer tailored advice specific to your needs, ensuring you maintain a balanced diet, optimize nutrition for exercise, and support overall health.

Nutrition is a vital component of your Wall Pilates journey. Embrace these nutritional guidelines as a supportive tool, empowering you to fuel your body effectively, optimize performance, aid recovery, and foster overall well-being.

Nutrition Advice	Description	Purpose
Balanced Meals	Ensure meals comprise a balance of macronutrients — proteins, carbohydrates, and healthy fats.	Supports overall energy levels, aids in muscle recovery, and provides essential nutrients for optimal performance during workouts.
Hydration Importance	Drink sufficient water throughout the day, especially before and after workouts.	Maintains hydration levels, supports bodily functions, aids in muscle function, and helps prevent fatigue during exercise.
Pre-Workout Fuel	Consume a light snack with a balance of carbohydrates and proteins about 30-60 minutes before a workout.	Provides a source of readily available energy, helps prevent hunger during exercise, and supports muscle maintenance.
Post-Workout Nutrition	Aim for a snack or meal containing carbohydrates and proteins within 30-60 minutes after exercising.	Assists in muscle recovery, replenishes glycogen stores, and aids in repair and growth of muscle tissue.
Healthy Snacking	Opt for nutrient-dense snacks like fruits, nuts, yogurt, or whole-grain crackers.	Provides sustained energy, curbs hunger between meals, and supplies essential vitamins and minerals.
Mindful Eating	Focus on portion control and mindful eating habits. Pay attention to hunger cues and avoid overeating.	Helps maintain a healthy weight, promotes digestion, and encourages appreciation of food without overindulgence.
Limit Processed Foods	Minimize intake of processed and sugary foods, opting for whole, natural foods instead.	Supports overall health, reduces inflammation, and provides more nutrients and fewer empty calories.
Balanced Diet Variety	Include a variety of foods from different food groups in meals.	Ensures intake of diverse nutrients, vitamins, and minerals essential for overall health and well-being.

Nutrition Advice	Description	Purpose
Quality Sleep	Adequate sleep is essential for recovery and overall health. Aim for 7-9 hours of quality sleep each night.	Supports muscle recovery, enhances mental focus, and aids in overall well-being, allowing the body to repair and recharge.
Consult a Professional	Consider consulting a registered dietitian or nutritionist for personalized guidance.	Provides tailored advice specific to individual needs, ensuring a balanced diet and optimal nutrition for exercise and health.

Chapter 2. MUSCLE GROUP EXERCISES

1. CORE STRENGTHENING EXERCISES

1. WALL CRUNCHES

Target Muscle Group: Abdominals

Not Recommended for: Individuals with severe lower back issues, herniated discs, or those experiencing discomfort during core engagement exercises.

INSTRUCTIONS:

1. **Starting Position:**
   Lie flat on your back with your glutes as close to the wall as comfortable. Extend your legs straight up against the wall. Place your hands behind your head, supporting your neck, and lift your shoulders slightly off the ground.

2. **Engage Core:**
   Lift your shoulders off the ground, contracting your abdominal muscles. Hold this position for 1-2 seconds, focusing on the contraction.

3. **Return to Starting Position:**
   Slowly lower your shoulders back down, returning to the starting position. Repeat the movement, maintaining control and engaging your core throughout.

4. **Duration:**
   Aim for 8-10 reps to start, focusing on quality over quantity.

COMPLICATIONS:

1. **For Beginners:** Avoid overarching the lower back; focus on keeping a gentle curvature without discomfort. Start with smaller motions and progress gradually.

2. **For Advanced:** To intensify, increase the number of repetitions or hold at the crunch position for longer durations.

HELPFUL HINT: Avoid pulling on your neck while performing the crunches. Focus on a controlled motion, emphasizing the contraction of the abdominal muscles. Start with a comfortable range of motion and gradually increase as your strength improves.

2. WALL PLANK VARIATIONS

Target Muscle Group: Core, Abdominals

Not Recommended for: Individuals with severe lower back issues, herniated discs, or discomfort during core engagement exercises.

INSTRUCTIONS:

1. **Starting Position:**
   Stand facing the wall at a comfortable distance allowing your back hands to touch it. Keep feet hip-width apart, firmly planted on the floor.

2. **Engage Core:**
   Pull your navel towards your spine, engaging your core without tensing your neck or shoulders excessively.

3. **Lift Off:**
   Gradually lift your feet a few inches off the ground, keeping your knees slightly bent.

4. **Plank Position:**
   Create a plank-like shape by ensuring your body forms a straight line from head to heels. Maintain a neutral spine without arching or sagging.

5. **Hold and Breathe:**
   Maintain this position, focusing on engaging your core muscles. Breathe steadily and avoid holding your breath.

6. **Duration:**
   Aim to hold this position for 20-30 seconds, gradually increasing the duration as you build strength.

COMPLICATIONS:

1. **For Beginners:** Avoid overarching or straining the lower back. Focus on maintaining a gentle plank position without discomfort.

2. **For Advanced:** Experiment with variations like lifting one leg or one arm at a time. Increase hold duration or add unstable surfaces to intensify the exercise.

HELPFUL HINT: Focus on maintaining proper form throughout the hold. If discomfort or strain occurs in your lower back or neck, regress the movement by reducing the lift or duration. Concentrate on maintaining a strong core engagement without compromising comfort.

3. WALL SIDE CRUNCHES

Target Muscle Group: Obliques, Core

Not Recommended for: Individuals with severe lower back issues, herniated discs, or acute discomfort during core exercises. Those experiencing acute neck or back pain during the movement.

INSTRUCTIONS:

1. **Starting Position:**
   Stand sideways to the wall, arm's length away. Your side should be facing the wall. Place one hand on the wall at shoulder height for support. Feet should be hip-width apart and firmly grounded.

2. **Engage Core:**
   Contract your abdominal muscles by pulling your navel towards your spine.

3. **Crunch Movement:**
   Exhale and slowly bring the bottom elbow up towards your hip, contracting the obliques on the side of the body facing away from the wall. Keep the movement controlled and avoid collapsing into the wall.

4. **Return to Starting:**
   Aim for 8-10 reps to start, focusing on quality over quantity.

5. **Repetitions:**
   Avoid over-exerting or straining the lower back. Focus on controlled movements; avoid any discomfort in the side body.

COMPLICATIONS:

1. **For Beginners:** Avoid overarching the lower back; focus on keeping a gentle curvature without discomfort. Start with smaller motions and progress gradually.

2. **For Advanced:** Increase the number of repetitions or incorporate variations like adding ankle weights or using a resistance band for added challenge.

HELPFUL HINT: Maintain a steady breathing pattern throughout the exercise. If you feel strain or discomfort, consider reducing the range of motion or the number of repetitions. Focus on engaging the side muscles without compromising comfort or form.

4. WALL SIT-UPS

Target Muscle Group: Core, Abdominals

Not Recommended for: Individuals with severe lower back issues, herniated discs, or discomfort during core engagement exercises. Anyone experiencing acute pain or strain in the neck or back.

INSTRUCTIONS:

1. **Starting Position:**
   Stand by the wall, ensuring your lower back can rest against it. Feet should be firmly planted hip-width apart on the floor.

2. **Engage Core:**
   Pull your navel towards your spine, engaging the core without straining your neck or shoulders.

3. **Movement:**
   Inhale deeply to prepare. As you exhale, contract your abdominal muscles and gradually slide down the wall. Articulate your spine, rolling down slowly until your lower back is flat against the wall.

4. **Sit-Up Position:**
   Hold the sit-up position for a moment, feeling the tension in your abdominal muscles.

5. **Return to Starting:**
   Inhale and slowly roll back up the wall, engaging your core and maintaining control.

6. **Repetitions:**
   Aim for 8-10 repetitions, focusing on controlled movement and engagement of the core throughout.

COMPLICATIONS:

1. **For Beginners:** Avoid overarching or straining the lower back. Focus on controlled movements without discomfort.

2. **For Advanced:** Increase the number of repetitions or add variations like holding a weight against your chest for added resistance.

HELPFUL HINT: Maintain a steady and controlled breathing pattern throughout the exercise. Avoid pulling on your neck or using momentum to lift your upper body. Focus on engaging the abdominal muscles to ensure effectiveness while minimizing strain on the neck and back.

5. WALL KNEE TUCKS

Target Muscle Group: Core, Abdominals

Not Recommended for: Individuals with severe lower back issues, herniated discs, or discomfort during core engagement exercises. Those experiencing acute pain or strain in the neck or back.

INSTRUCTIONS:

1. **Starting Position:**
   Stand facing the wall with your feet firmly planted on the floor, balancing on your toes and keeping them hip-width apart.

2. **Engage Core:**
   Pull your navel towards your spine, engaging the core without straining your neck or shoulders.

3. **Movement:**
   Inhale deeply to prepare. As you exhale, contract your abdominal muscles and gradually lift your knees towards your chest. Aim to bring your knees as close to your chest as comfortable without straining.

4. **Hold and Lower:**
   Hold the tucked position for a moment, feeling the engagement in your core. Inhale and slowly lower your feet back to the starting position.

5. **Repetitions:**
   Aim for 8-10 repetitions, focusing on controlled movement and engagement of the core throughout.

COMPLICATIONS:

1. **For Beginners:** Avoid overarching or straining the lower back. Focus on controlled movements without discomfort.

2. **For Advanced:** Increase the number of repetitions or incorporate variations like holding the tucked position for longer or increasing the speed of tucks.

HELPFUL HINT: Focus on quality over quantity; maintain proper form throughout the movement. If you experience discomfort or strain in your lower back or neck, reduce the range of motion or pace of the movement. Prioritize maintaining a strong core engagement without compromising your comfort.

6. WALL LEG RAISES

Target Muscle Group: Core, Lower Abdominals

Not Recommended for: Individuals with severe lower back issues, herniated discs, or discomfort during core engagement exercises. Those experiencing acute pain or strain in the neck, back, or lower abdomen.

INSTRUCTIONS:

1. **Starting Position:**
   Stand by the wall, ensuring your back rests against it. Feet should be hip-width apart, firmly planted on the floor.

2. **Engage Core:**
   Pull your navel towards your spine, engaging the core without straining your neck or shoulders excessively.

3. **Leg Raise:**
   Inhale deeply. As you exhale, slowly lift one leg in front of you while keeping the other firmly on the ground. Aim to raise your leg to a comfortable height, focusing on engaging the lower abdominal muscles.

4. **Hold and Lower:**
   Hold the raised leg for a moment, feeling the engagement in your lower abs. Inhale and slowly lower your leg back to the starting position.

5. **Repetitions:**
   Perform 8-10 repetitions per leg, maintaining controlled movement and engagement of the core throughout.

COMPLICATIONS:

1. **For Beginners:** Avoid overarching or straining the lower back; focus on controlled movements without discomfort. Gradually increase the range of motion as strength and flexibility improve.

2. **For Advanced:** Increase the number of repetitions or incorporate variations like ankle weights or slow, controlled movements for an added challenge.

HELPFUL HINT: Focus on maintaining proper form throughout the movement. If you experience discomfort or strain in your lower back or neck, reduce the range of motion or pace of the movement. Prioritize maintaining a strong core engagement without compromising your comfort.

7. CALF RAISE WALL SIT

Target Muscle Group: Calves, Quadriceps

Not Recommended for: Individuals with severe knee issues, joint problems, or recent lower body injuries. Avoid if you experience discomfort in the knees or lower body during squats.

INSTRUCTIONS:

1. **Starting Position:**
   Stand with your back against a wall or sturdy surface, feet shoulder-width apart, and approximately 1.5 to 2 feet away from the wall. Squat down, ensuring your knees form a 90-degree angle. Your back should be against the wall, and your weight evenly distributed on both feet.

2. **Calf Raise:**
   Raise your heels off the ground, shifting your weight onto the balls of your feet or tiptoes.Hold this raised position for 5-10 seconds, feeling the contraction in your calves and quads.

3. **Return to Squat Position:**
   Lower your heels back down, returning to the starting squat position. Repeat the movement, maintaining control and focusing on engaging your calf muscles throughout.

4. **Repetition and Duration:**
   Aim to perform 8-12 repetitions, gradually increasing as you become more comfortable with the movement.

COMPLICATIONS:

1. **For Beginners:** Begin with a shallower squat, ensuring your knees remain at a comfortable angle without straining. Initially, focus on shorter hold durations and gradually increase as you gain strength.

2. **For Advanced:** To intensify, increase the duration of the hold or add weights by holding dumbbells.

HELPFUL HINT: Keep your back against the wall throughout the exercise. Start with a shorter hold duration, ensuring you feel comfortable and gradually increase the hold time as your calf and quad strength improves. Avoid locking your knees or leaning too far forward during the movement to prevent unnecessary strain on your lower body.

8. WALL RUSSIAN TWISTS

Target Muscle Group: Obliques, Core

Not Recommended for: Individuals with acute back pain, spinal injuries, or those unable to maintain proper form during twisting movements.

INSTRUCTIONS:

1. **Starting Position:**
Stand with your back against a wall, feet shoulder-width apart, and slightly away from the wall. Lower into a squat position until your thighs are parallel to the floor, keeping your back against the wall for support.

2. **Engage Core:**
Draw your navel in towards your spine to engage your core muscles, maintaining a neutral spine.

3. **Twisting Movement:**
Keeping your hands lightly touching the wall for balance, twist your torso to the right, leading with your chest. Keep your hips square and avoid shifting your weight to one side.

4. **Return:**
Slowly reverse the twist, bringing your torso back to center, then repeat the twist to the left side. Continue alternating twists for the desired number of repetitions.

5. **Breathing Technique:**
Inhale as you center, exhale as you twist, maintaining steady breathing throughout the movement.

6. **Repetition and Duration:**
Aim to perform 8-12 repetitions on each side, gradually increasing as you become more comfortable with the movement.

COMPLICATIONS:

1. **For Beginners:** Ensure proper alignment of the spine and hips throughout the movement. Focus on controlled twisting without compromising balance.

2. **For Advanced:** Increase the intensity by holding a light weight or medicine ball at chest level while performing the twists. This adds resistance and challenges core stability.

HELPFUL HINT: Focus on maintaining stability through the lower body while engaging the obliques to execute the twist. Keep the movement controlled and avoid jerking or over-rotating to prevent strain on the spine.

9. WALL BRIDGE

Target Muscle Group: Glutes, Hamstrings, Lower Back

Not Recommended for: Individuals with acute back issues, severe spinal injuries, or those experiencing discomfort in the lower back during hip extension exercises.

INSTRUCTIONS:

1. **Starting Position:**
   Lie on your back with your arms by your sides. Position your feet hip-width apart, pressing the soles against a wall. Bend your knees at a 90-degree angle, ensuring your thighs are perpendicular to the floor.

2. **Bridge Movement:**
   Engage your glutes and core muscles, then lift your hips off the ground as high as comfortable, forming a straight line from your shoulders to your knees. Squeeze your glutes at the top of the movement, holding the raised position for a moment.

3. **Return to Start:**
   Gradually lower your hips back to the starting position, ensuring controlled movement and maintaining the engagement of your glutes and core. Repeat the movement for the desired number of repetitions or duration.

4. **Repetition and Duration:**
   Aim to perform 8-12 repetitions, gradually increasing as you become more comfortable with the movement.

COMPLICATIONS:

1. **For Beginners:** Initially, focus on smaller hip lifts to avoid strain or discomfort in the lower back. Ensure your feet are comfortably planted on the wall and maintain a controlled movement throughout.

2. **For Advanced:** To increase difficulty, hold the raised position for a longer duration or elevate one leg while lifting the hips.

HELPFUL HINT: Ensure a steady and controlled movement throughout the exercise, avoiding overarching or excessive strain in the lower back. Focus on engaging the glutes and maintaining a stable bridge position. If you experience discomfort or strain in your lower back, reduce the range of motion or consult with a fitness professional for modifications.

CORE STRENGTHENING EXERCISES

1. WALL CRUNCHES

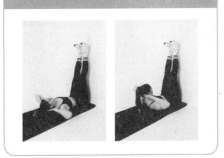

2. WALL PLANK VARIATIONS

3. WALL SIDE CRUNCHES

4. WALL SIT-UPS

5. WALL KNEE TUCKS

6. WALL LEG RAISES

7. CALF RAISE WALL SIT

8. WALL RUSSIAN TWISTS

9. WALL BRIDGE

2. UPPER BODY TONING EXERCISES

1. WALL PUSH-UPS

Target Muscle Group: Upper Body (Chest, Shoulders, Triceps)

Not Recommended for: Individuals with shoulder or wrist injuries, and those experiencing acute pain in the wrists, shoulders, or back.

INSTRUCTIONS:

1. **Starting Position:**
   Stand facing the wall at an arm's length distance. Place your hands flat against the wall, slightly wider than shoulder-width apart, at shoulder level.

2. **Body Alignment:**
   Ensure your body forms a straight line from head to heels, engaging your core muscles for stability.

3. **Execution:**
   Bend your elbows, lowering your body towards the wall. Keep your body in a straight line and lower until your chest almost touches the wall.

4. **Push Back:**
   Push through your palms, straightening your elbows to return to the starting position. Maintain control and avoid locking your elbows at the top.

5. **Repetitions:**
   Aim for 8-12 reps initially, adjusting based on your comfort level and strength.

COMPLICATIONS:

1. **For Beginners:** Avoid overarching the lower back or putting excessive strain on the wrists. Focus on maintaining a straight body line and controlled movements.

2. **For Advanced:** To increase difficulty, consider doing inclined push-ups by gradually moving your feet farther from the wall or doing diamond-shaped hand placements to focus more on triceps.

HELPFUL HINT: Keep your wrists aligned with your shoulders, and maintain a controlled breathing pattern. Focus on engaging the chest and shoulder muscles during the movement, avoiding any strain on the wrists and maintaining proper form.

2. WALL ANGELS

Target Muscle Group: Upper Back, Shoulders

Not Recommended for: Individuals with shoulder or neck injuries, severe limitations in shoulder mobility, or those unable to maintain proper form due to physical constraints.

INSTRUCTIONS:

1. **Starting Position:**
   Stand with your back against the wall, feet positioned 6-12 inches away, knees slightly bent, and mid-back flattened against the wall. Tuck your chin slightly, lengthening the neck, and place the back of your head, elbows, and hands against the wall. Shoulders should be away from the ears.

2. **Wall Angels:**
   Start with arms in a "V" position angle, elbows and backs of hands against the wall. Slowly straighten your arms overhead, maintaining contact with the wall using your entire back, head, elbows, and hands. Ensure shoulder blades stay down during the movement, keeping the motion slow and controlled.

3. **Return to Start:**
   Gradually return to the initial position, maintaining contact with the wall at all times. Perform the exercise for the desired number of repetitions without compromising form.

4. **Repetitions:**
   Aim for 8-10 reps to start, focusing on quality over quantity.

COMPLICATIONS:

1. **For Beginners:** Initiate the movement with smaller ranges of motion, focusing on maintaining contact with the wall throughout the exercise. Ensure a posterior pelvic tilt and engage the mid-back against the wall without overarching the lower back.

2. **For Advanced:** To intensify, increase the time spent in the "Y" position or add lightweight resistance for the arms, ensuring smooth and controlled movement.

HELPFUL HINT: Focus on smooth and controlled movements throughout. Keep the entire back, head, elbows, and hands in contact with the wall during the full range of motion. Gradually increase the range or add minimal resistance as you progress, ensuring proper engagement and no strain in the shoulders or neck.

3. WALL SHOULDER TAPS

Target Muscle Group: Shoulders, Core

Not Recommended for: Individuals with shoulder or wrist injuries, and those experiencing acute pain or discomfort in the shoulder or core area.

INSTRUCTIONS:

1. **Starting Position:**
   Begin in a plank position, facing the wall and at an arm's length distance. Place your hands on the wall at shoulder height, slightly wider than shoulder-width apart.

2. **Execution:**
   Engage your core and shoulders, then lift one hand off the wall, tapping the opposite shoulder. Return the hand to the initial position and alternate sides in a controlled manner.

3. **Tap Sequence:**
   Tap each shoulder alternatively, focusing on keeping the hips stable and minimizing swaying or rotation of the torso.

4. **Repetitions:**
   Aim for 10-12 taps on each shoulder to start, gradually increasing as you gain comfort and strength.

COMPLICATIONS:

1. **For Beginners:** Start slow to maintain stability. Keep your core engaged to avoid swaying and maintain control throughout the exercise.

2. **For Advanced:** To increase difficulty, try performing the taps at a faster pace while ensuring proper form and stability. You can also add a push-up between taps for a more challenging variation.

HELPFUL HINT: Maintain a strong plank position throughout the exercise. Avoid hunching or rounding the upper back, and focus on engaging the core and shoulder muscles to stabilize the body. Control the movement and avoid rushing to tap the shoulders, prioritizing proper form over speed.

4. WALL CHEST PRESS

Target Muscle Group: Chest, Arms, Shoulders

Not Recommended for: Individuals with shoulder, elbow, or wrist injuries, or those who experience discomfort in the chest or shoulder areas during movement.

INSTRUCTIONS:

1. **Starting Position:**
   Stand facing the wall, about an arm's length away. Place your hands flat against the wall at shoulder height, slightly wider than shoulder-width apart. Keep your feet comfortably planted on the floor, hip-width apart.

2. **Execution:**
   Inhale deeply to prepare. As you exhale, slowly bend your elbows, bringing your chest towards the wall, maintaining a straight line from head to heels.

3. **Press Movement:**
   Push back against the wall, extending your arms fully but without locking your elbows. Engage your chest muscles during the press, ensuring control throughout the movement.

4. **Repetitions:**
   Aim for 10-15 repetitions to start, gradually increasing as you become more comfortable with the exercise.

COMPLICATIONS:

1. **For Beginners:** Focus on control and proper form. Ensure the wrists are in line with the elbows and shoulders to avoid strain.

2. **For Advanced:** To increase difficulty, consider adding resistance bands around the arms or using different hand positions, such as closer together or wider apart, to engage different parts of the chest and arms.

HELPFUL HINT: Maintain a neutral spine and engage your core muscles to stabilize your body. Focus on controlled movements while pressing against the wall and returning to the starting position. Avoid arching your back or shrugging your shoulders during the exercise. Ensure your body remains aligned from head to toe throughout the movement.

5. WALL TRICEP DIPS

Target Muscle Group: Triceps, Shoulders

Not Recommended for: Individuals with existing shoulder or elbow injuries, chronic shoulder pain, or instability issues in the wrists or shoulders. Avoid this exercise if experiencing acute discomfort in the wrists, elbows, or shoulders.

INSTRUCTIONS:

1. **Starting Position:**
   Stand facing away from the wall, about an arm's length away. Place your hands flat against the wall at shoulder-width apart, shoulder height or slightly lower. Keep your feet comfortably planted on the floor, hip-width apart.

2. **Execution:**
   Inhale deeply to prepare. As you exhale, bend your elbows, lowering your body towards the wall while maintaining a straight line from head to heels.

3. **Dip Movement:**
   Lower your body by bending your elbows, keeping them close to your sides. Ensure your shoulders remain stable without rolling forward. Your chest should gently graze the wall without touching it.

4. **Press Movement:**
   Push back against the wall, extending your arms without locking your elbows. Engage your triceps and press your body back to the starting position.

5. **Repetitions:**
   Aim for 8-12 repetitions, adjusting as necessary based on your comfort and strength level.

COMPLICATIONS:

1. **For Beginners:** Focus on maintaining controlled movement and avoiding excessive strain on the shoulders and wrists. Start with a comfortable range of motion.

2. **For Advanced:** To increase difficulty, consider elevating the feet on a raised surface or using a lower wall to deepen the dip angle, increasing the resistance on the triceps.

HELPFUL HINT: Maintain a neutral spine, avoid overarching your back, and engage your core muscles throughout the movement. Focus on controlled dips, ensuring the elbows track backward, not flaring out to the sides. Control the descent and ascent to work the triceps effectively while minimizing strain on the shoulders and wrists.

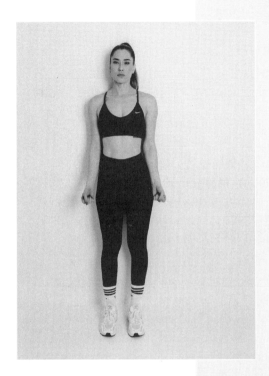

6. WALL BICEP CURLS

Target Muscle Group: Biceps

Not Recommended for: Individuals with acute or chronic elbow, wrist, or shoulder injuries. It's crucial to avoid this exercise if experiencing any pain or discomfort in these areas.

INSTRUCTIONS:

1. **Starting Position:**
   Stand with your back against the wall, ensuring your entire spine touches the surface. Feet should be hip-width apart, placed about a foot away from the wall. Keep your core engaged for stability.

2. **Arm Position:**
   Extend your arms fully down, palms facing forward, against the wall. Elbows should be close to your sides and slightly bent.

3. **Curling Movement:**
   While keeping your upper arms still, exhale and slowly bend your elbows, bringing your palms towards your shoulders. Focus on contracting your biceps.

4. **Peak Contractions:**
   Once your palms reach your shoulders, pause briefly, feeling the contraction in your biceps.

5. **Return to Start:**
   Inhale and slowly lower your arms back to the starting position, ensuring controlled movement throughout.

6. **Repetitions:**
   Aim for 10-15 repetitions, adjusting based on your comfort level and maintaining proper form.

COMPLICATIONS:

1. **For Beginners:** Focus on maintaining proper form throughout the exercise. Start with a light resistance level or bodyweight and gradually progress.

   For Advanced: To intensify, consider using resistance bands or weights while performing the curls. Variations like slowing down the movement or adding isometric holds at the peak can also increase difficulty.

HELPFUL HINT: Ensure your elbows remain stationary against the wall throughout the movement. Maintain a controlled pace and avoid using momentum to lift your arms. Focus on the engagement of the biceps and avoid excessive strain on the elbows or wrists. For increased effectiveness, emphasize the mind-muscle connection, focusing on the bicep contraction during the upward movement.

7. WALL PLANK WITH ARM REACH

Target Muscle Group: Core, Shoulders, Arms

Not Recommended for: Individuals with shoulder or wrist injuries. Avoid if experiencing acute pain in the wrists, shoulders, or upper body.

INSTRUCTIONS:

1. **Starting Position:**
   Stand facing the wall, maintaining a comfortable distance. Lean forward and place your hands on the wall, slightly wider than shoulder-width apart. Walk your feet back until your body forms a straight line from head to heels.

2. **Plank Position:**
   Engage your core muscles and maintain a straight line from head to heels, avoiding any sagging or arching in your lower back.

3. **Arm Reach:**
   While keeping the plank position stable, lift one hand off the wall and reach forward, extending your leg parallel to the ground.

4. **Return to Starting Position:**
   Bring your hand back to the wall and place it down before repeating the movement with the opposite arm.

5. **Alternate Arms:**
   Continue alternating arm and leg reaches while maintaining a stable plank position.

6. **Repetitions and Duration:**
   Aim for 8-10 reaches per arm, focusing on stability and control.

COMPLICATIONS:

1. **For Beginners:** Focus on maintaining proper form throughout the exercise. Begin with shorter holds and gradually progress to longer durations.

2. **For Advanced:** To increase difficulty, you can incorporate variations such as lifting one leg, adding a push-up after the reach, or using ankle weights for added resistance.

HELPFUL HINT: Keep your core engaged throughout the exercise to stabilize your body. Focus on maintaining a strong and stable plank position without allowing your hips to sag or rise. Ensure controlled movements during the arm reaches, avoiding any excessive twisting or shifting of the body. Focus on maintaining a smooth, controlled breathing pattern throughout the exercise.

8. WALL WRIST FLEXOR STRETCH

Target Muscle Group: Forearms, Wrist Flexors

Not Recommended for: Individuals with existing wrist injuries, recent surgeries, or severe wrist pain. Avoid if experiencing acute discomfort or pain during the stretch.

 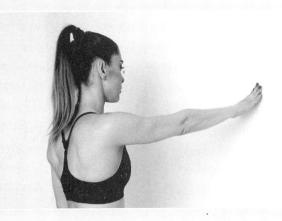

INSTRUCTIONS:

1. **Starting Position:**
   Stand facing the wall, maintaining a comfortable distance.

2. **Hand Placement:**
   Place your palm against the wall.

3. **Stretching Movement:**
   Gently press your palm and fingers against the wall while maintaining a straight arm. You should feel a stretch along the forearm and wrist.

4. **Adjusting Intensity:**
   To intensify the stretch, slightly lean your body forward, keeping your arm straight. Adjust the angle of your hand against the wall to find the most comfortable yet effective stretch.

5. **Duration:**
   Hold the stretch for 20-30 seconds while breathing steadily. Repeat the stretch on the other arm.

COMPLICATIONS:

1. **For Beginners:** Start with gentle stretches and gradually increase the stretch as your flexibility improves. Avoid excessive force during the stretch to prevent strain.

2. **For Advanced:** To deepen the stretch, lean your body slightly forward while maintaining proper form. Additionally, using a different hand position against the wall can alter the stretch intensity.

HELPFUL HINT: Focus on maintaining a relaxed, steady breath throughout the stretch. Avoid bouncing or forcing the stretch; instead, aim for a comfortable stretch that gradually improves over time. If you feel any pain or discomfort, ease off the stretch immediately. Regularly performing this stretch can help improve wrist flexibility and reduce tension in the forearm muscles.

9. WALL WRIST EXTENSOR STRETCH

Target Muscle Group: Forearms, Wrist Extensors

Not Recommended for: Individuals with recent wrist injuries, surgeries, acute wrist pain, or any discomfort that worsens with this stretch.

INSTRUCTIONS:

1. **Starting Position:**
   Stand facing a wall, maintaining a distance where you can comfortably extend your arm.

2. **Hand Placement:**
   Extend your arm straight in front of you, parallel to the ground, and place the back of your hand against the wall, fingers pointing downward.

3. **Stretching Movement:**
   Gently press the back of your hand against the wall while keeping your arm straight. You should feel a stretch along the top of your forearm and wrist.

4. **Adjusting Intensity:**
   To deepen the stretch, slightly adjust the angle of your hand or lean your body forward, maintaining a comfortable position. Avoid forcing the stretch or causing discomfort.

5. **Duration:**
   Hold the stretch for 20-30 seconds while maintaining a steady breathing pattern. Switch to the other arm and repeat the stretch.

COMPLICATIONS:

1. **For Beginners:** Start with gentle stretches and gradually increase the stretch as your flexibility improves. Avoid applying excessive pressure to the wrist joint or stretching to the point of pain.

2. **For Advanced:** To intensify the stretch, experiment with slight variations in hand placement or increase the duration of the stretch gradually.

HELPFUL HINT: Focus on gradual and controlled movements, avoiding sudden or forceful stretches that could strain the wrist. Only stretch to the point of mild tension, never to the point of pain. Consistency in performing this stretch can improve wrist flexibility and alleviate tension in the forearm muscles over time.

UPPER BODY TONING EXERCISES

1. WALL PUSH-UPS

2. WALL ANGELS

3. WALL SHOULDER TAPS

4. WALL CHEST PRESS

5. WALL TRICEP DIPS

6. WALL BICEP CURLS

7. WALL PLANK WITH ARM REACH

8. WALL WRIST FLEXOR STRETCH

9. WALL WRIST EXTENSOR STRETCH

3. LOWER BODY CONDITIONING EXERCISES

1. WALL SQUATS

Target Muscle Group: Quadriceps, Hamstrings, Glutes

Not Recommended for: Individuals with knee injuries, recent knee surgeries, or severe discomfort in the knees. Avoid this exercise if it exacerbates knee pain.

INSTRUCTIONS:

1. **Starting Position:**
   Stand with your back against a wall, keeping your back straight, feet hip-width apart, and approximately 1-2 feet away from the wall. Engage your core.

2. **Squatting Movement:**
   Lower your body by bending your knees and hips, as if sitting back into an imaginary chair. Slide down the wall, keeping your back straight until your thighs are parallel to the floor.

3. **Positioning:**
   Ensure your knees are aligned with your ankles and not extending past your toes. Your back should remain in contact with the wall, and your feet planted firmly on the floor.

4. **Hold:**
   Maintain the squat position for 20-30 seconds or as long as comfortable, focusing on steady breathing.

5. **Rise:**
   Push through your heels, engaging your quadriceps and hamstrings, to return to the starting position.

COMPLICATIONS:

1. **For Beginners:** Start with partial squats, focusing on form and avoiding excessive depth. Gradually increase the depth as strength and flexibility improve.

2. **For Advanced:** Enhance difficulty by holding the squat position for an extended duration or adding resistance like holding a medicine ball against the chest or using ankle weights.

HELPFUL HINT: Focus on maintaining proper form throughout the exercise. Avoid letting your knees cave inward and ensure your back stays against the wall. Gradually increase the depth of the squat as your strength and flexibility improve. Wall squats are an effective lower body exercise that enhances leg strength and stability while minimizing stress on the knees.

2. WALL LUNGES

Target Muscle Group: Quadriceps, Hamstrings, Glutes

Not Recommended for: Individuals with knee or hip injuries, recent surgeries, or severe discomfort in these areas. Avoid this exercise if it exacerbates knee or hip pain.

INSTRUCTIONS:

1. **Starting Position:**
   Stand facing the wall, about an arm's length away. Keep your feet shoulder-width apart and rest your hands on the wall for balance.

2. **Lunging Movement:**
   Take a step back with one foot, lowering your body into a lunge position. Bend both knees, ensuring the front knee stays aligned with the ankle and doesn't extend past the toes.

3. **Positioning:**
   Lower your body until the back knee almost touches the ground, aiming for a 90-degree angle with both knees. Maintain an upright torso throughout the movement.

4. **Hold:**
   Hold the lunge position for 10-20 seconds, focusing on stability and balance.

5. **Return:**
   Push through the front heel to return to the starting position. Alternate between legs, performing the same movement on the opposite side.

6. **Repetitions:**
   Aim for 8-10 reps to start, focusing on quality over quantity.

COMPLICATIONS:

1. **For Beginners:** Start with shallow lunges, ensuring your knee does not extend past your toes. Focus on balance and stability before attempting deeper lunges.

2. **For Advanced:** Increase difficulty by performing deeper lunges or incorporating variations such as holding weights or increasing the lunge duration.

HELPFUL HINT: Focus on maintaining proper form — avoid letting the front knee extend beyond the toes and keep your back straight. Gradually increase the depth of the lunge as you gain strength and balance. Wall lunges are effective for targeting the lower body muscles while emphasizing stability and balance.

3. WALL LEG PRESS

Target Muscle Group: Quadriceps, Hamstrings, Glutes

Not Recommended for: Individuals with knee injuries, severe discomfort, or recent knee surgeries. Avoid this exercise if it causes acute knee pain or discomfort.

INSTRUCTIONS:

1. **Starting Position:**
   Stand by the wall, maintaining a distance of about two feet away. Keep your feet shoulder-width apart and flat on the floor.

2. **Pressing Movement:**
   Lean against the wall, ensuring your lower back is in contact with the surface. Gently bend your knees and slide down the wall until they reach a 90-degree angle.

3. **Press:**
   Slowly press through your heels to extend your legs, pushing your body back up the wall. Ensure the movement is controlled and steady.

4. **Hold:**
   Once your legs are extended, hold the position for a few seconds, engaging your quadriceps and glutes. Hold this position for X number of breaths (more = harder). Visualize pushing the floor away from you as you SLOWLY stand up tall. Push evenly through your whole foot (heals to toes) as you rise up.

5. **Return:**
   Gradually bend your knees, lowering your body back down the wall to the starting position. Repeat the same with the other leg.

6. **Repetitions:**
   Aim for 8-10 reps to start, focusing on quality over quantity.

COMPLICATIONS:

1. **For Beginners:** Start with shallow leg presses, ensuring the knees don't extend past the toes. Focus on form and control before increasing depth.

   For Advanced: To increase difficulty, perform deeper leg presses or add resistance by using ankle weights or resistance bands.

HELPFUL HINT: Keep your feet flat on the ground and avoid letting your knees extend past your toes. Focus on the engagement of the quadriceps and glutes throughout the movement. Start with a shallow range of motion and gradually increase depth as your strength and flexibility improve.

4. WALL CALF RAISES

Target Muscle Group: Calves

Not Recommended for: Individuals with severe ankle or foot injuries, Achilles tendon issues, or those experiencing acute pain or discomfort in the ankles or calves.

INSTRUCTIONS:

1. **Starting Position:**
   Stand facing the wall with your feet hip-width apart and about a foot away from the wall. Ensure your posture is upright, and your core is engaged.

2. **Rise onto Toes:**
   Slowly lift your heels off the ground, rising onto the balls of your feet, pushing through the balls of your feet and toes.

3. **Hold:**
   At the top of the movement, pause for a moment, feeling the contraction in your calf muscles.

4. **Lower:**
   Gradually lower your heels back to the floor, maintaining control and ensuring a smooth descent.

5. **Repeat:**
   Repeat the motion for the desired number of repetitions, focusing on maintaining stability and control throughout.

COMPLICATIONS:

1. **For Beginners:** Start with a partial range of motion, raising your heels only a few inches off the ground to avoid strain. Focus on stability and control.

2. **For Advanced:** Increase the difficulty by performing full-range calf raises or holding weights against your thighs for added resistance.

HELPFUL HINT: Keep your movements controlled and avoid bouncing at the bottom or top of the movement. Gradually increase the range of motion as your strength improves. Focus on the engagement of the calf muscles and maintain steady breathing throughout the exercise.

5. WALL HAMSTRING CURLS

Target Muscle Group: Hamstrings

Not Recommended for: Individuals with acute knee injuries, instability, or pain during knee flexion exercises.

INSTRUCTIONS:

1. **Starting Position:**
   Maintain an upright posture by utilizing a wall for stability as you stand on one leg.

2. **Engage Core:**
   Brace your core to stabilize your torso and maintain proper posture throughout the movement.

3. **Hamstring Curl:**
   Slowly and smoothly lift your heel towards your buttocks, feeling the contraction in your hamstring muscles. Keep the movement controlled, aiming to take at least 5 seconds to lift and lower the heel.

4. **Lower Leg:**
   Slowly lower your foot back to the starting position, maintaining control and focusing on the eccentric phase of the movement.

5. **Alternate Legs:**
   Repeat the movement on the opposite leg, lifting and lowering the heel with the same controlled motion.

6. **Repetitions:**
   Aim to perform 8-12 repetitions on each leg, focusing on quality rather than quantity.

COMPLICATIONS:

1. **For Beginners:** Start with a small range of motion and gradually increase as you build strength and flexibility in the hamstrings. Focus on maintaining proper alignment and avoid arching the lower back.

2. **For Advanced:** To increase difficulty, perform the exercise with both legs simultaneously or add ankle weights for added resistance.

HELPFUL HINT: Keep your knees close together and avoid swinging the leg or using momentum to lift the heel. Focus on feeling the muscles working throughout the movement and maintain a steady pace to maximize the effectiveness of the exercise.

6. WALL SIDE LEG LIFTS

Target Muscle Group: Abductors (Outer Thigh Muscles)

Not Recommended for: Individuals with acute hip or knee injuries or those experiencing discomfort while performing leg abduction movements.

INSTRUCTIONS:

1. **Starting Position:**
   Stand sideways next to the wall, keeping your hand lightly touching the wall for support. Feet should be together, and your body should be in a straight line.

2. **Leg Lift:**
   Lift your top leg away from the wall, keeping it straight or slightly bent, leading with your heel. Lift the leg to the height that is comfortable for you.

3. **Hold and Lower:**
   Pause momentarily at the top of the movement, feeling the contraction in your outer thigh, then slowly lower the leg back down without letting it touch the bottom leg.

4. **Maintain Control:**
   Ensure that the movement is controlled throughout, avoiding any jerky or abrupt motions.

5. **Repetitions:**
   Aim to perform 8-12 repetitions on each leg, focusing on quality rather than quantity.

COMPLICATIONS:

1. **For Beginners:** Start with a smaller range of motion and avoid lifting the leg too high to prevent strain on the hips and maintain balance.

2. **For Advanced:** Increase difficulty by extending the top leg fully or adding ankle weights to intensify resistance.

HELPFUL HINT: Maintain proper posture throughout the exercise. Focus on engaging the outer thigh muscles to lift the leg rather than using momentum. Start with a small range of motion and gradually increase it as you gain strength and stability.

7. WALL HIP ABDUCTION

Target Muscle Group: Hip Abductors (Outer Hip Muscles)

Not Recommended for: Individuals with acute hip or knee injuries, instability, or discomfort while performing hip abduction movements.

INSTRUCTIONS:

1. **Starting Position:**
   Stand sideways next to the wall, keeping your hand lightly touching the wall for support. Feet should be together, and your body should be in a straight line.

2. **Leg Lift:**
   Lift your top leg away from the wall, keeping it straight or slightly bent, leading with your heel. Lift the leg to the height that is comfortable for you.

3. **Hold and Lower:**
   Pause momentarily at the top of the movement, feeling the contraction in your outer hip, then slowly lower the leg back down without letting it touch the bottom leg.

4. **Maintain Control:**
   Ensure that the movement is controlled throughout, avoiding any jerky or abrupt motions.

5. **Repetitions:**
   Aim to perform 8-12 repetitions on each leg.

COMPLICATIONS:

1. **For Beginners:** Start with a smaller range of motion and avoid lifting the leg too high to prevent strain on the hips and maintain balance.

   For Advanced: Increase difficulty by extending the top leg fully or adding ankle weights to intensify resistance.

HELPFUL HINT: Maintain proper posture throughout the exercise. Focus on engaging the outer hip muscles to lift the leg rather than using momentum. Start with a small range of motion and gradually increase it as you gain strength and stability.

8. WALL HIP HINGE

Target Muscle Group: Glutes, Hamstrings

Not Recommended for: Individuals with acute hip or knee injuries, or those with limited mobility in the lower body.

INSTRUCTIONS:

1. **Starting Position:**
   Stand with your feet shoulder-width apart, approximately 6-12 inches away from a wall. Ensure your back is straight, chest lifted, and shoulders relaxed.

2. **Hip Hinge:**
   Initiate the movement by hinging at your hips, as if you were closing a car door with your buttocks, and gently lean backward until your buttocks touch the wall. Maintain a slight bend in your knees throughout the movement.

3. **Pause and Engage:**
   Once your buttocks touch the wall, pause briefly to feel the engagement in your glutes and hamstrings. Focus on maintaining a strong core and neutral spine alignment.

4. **Return to Starting Position:**
   Slowly and with control, return to an upright standing position by reversing the hip hinge movement. Keep your chest tall and shoulders relaxed as you return to the starting position.

5. **Repetitions:**
   Aim to complete 2 sets of 10-15 repetitions, performing the exercise 2-3 times a day for optimal results.

COMPLICATIONS:

1. **For Beginners:** Begin with a small range of motion and focus on mastering the technique before increasing intensity. Avoid overarching the lower back and maintain a slight bend in the knees throughout the movement.

2. **For Advanced:** To enhance the challenge, hold onto a weight or resistance band for added resistance, or increase the range of motion by hinging further at the hips.

HELPFUL HINT: Maintain proper posture throughout the exercise. Focus on engaging the outer thigh muscles to lift the leg rather than using momentum. Start with a small range of motion and gradually increase it as you gain strength and stability.

9. WALL KNEE EXTENSIONS

Target Muscle Group: Quadriceps (Front thigh muscles)

Not Recommended for: Individuals with knee issues, recent knee surgeries, or those experiencing discomfort or pain during knee extension movements.

INSTRUCTIONS:

1. **Starting Position:**
   Stand with your back to the wall, maintaining a distance of about an arm's length. Lean against the wall with your back, ensuring your lower back is flat against the surface. Your feet should be positioned hip-width apart, comfortably away from the wall.

2. **Execution:**
   Gradually slide your back down the wall, bending your knees slightly. Engage your core by gently pulling your navel towards your spine.

3. **Knee Extension:**
   Lift one leg, extending the knee fully without locking it, and then slowly lower it back down. Repeat the movement with the other leg.

4. **Controlled Movement:**
   Ensure a controlled and deliberate motion throughout, avoiding rapid or jerky movements.

5. **Repetitions:**
   Aim for 8-10 reps to start, focusing on quality over quantity.

COMPLICATIONS:

1. **For Beginners:** Start with small knee movements, avoiding overextension, to prevent strain on the knee joints.

   For Advanced: To increase difficulty, consider incorporating ankle weights or resistance bands around the lower thighs.

HELPFUL HINT: Maintain proper posture and control during the exercise. Avoid locking the knees at the top of the movement. Initiate the movement with a smaller range of motion and gradually increase as comfort and stability improve. Focus on engaging the quadriceps muscles while extending the knee.

10. WALL HIP FLEXOR STRETCH

Target Muscle Group: Hip flexors (Front of the hip)

Not Recommended for: Individuals with severe hip injuries, recent hip surgeries, or acute pain in the hip area.

INSTRUCTIONS:

1. **Starting Position:**
   Stand facing away from the wall, about an arm's length away. Place your hands on the wall at shoulder height for support.

2. **Stretch Execution:**
   Take a step back with one foot, allowing the heel of the rear foot to remain on the ground. The other leg is forward with the knee bent at a 90-degree angle, positioned directly above the ankle.

   Keep the back leg straight and engage the glutes while gently pressing the hips forward. You should feel a stretch along the front of the hip of the back leg.

3. **Hold & Breathe:**
   Hold the stretch for 20-30 seconds while maintaining steady breathing.

4. **Switch Sides:**
   Repeat the stretch on the opposite side.

COMPLICATIONS:

1. **For Beginners:** Start with a mild stretch, gradually increasing intensity as comfort improves. Avoid overstretching the muscles, which may cause discomfort.

2. **For Advanced:** To deepen the stretch, lift the back foot slightly off the ground while maintaining balance. A more advanced variation includes reaching the arms overhead while in the stretch position.

HELPFUL HINT: Maintain proper posture throughout the stretch. Avoid overarching the lower back; keep the torso upright and engage the core muscles. Gradually increase the stretch without pushing to the point of pain. Focus on breathing deeply and relaxing into the stretch to improve flexibility in the hip flexors.

LOWER BODY CONDITIONING EXERCISES

1. WALL SQUATS

2. WALL LUNGES

3. WALL LEG PRESS

4. WALL CALF RAISES

5. WALL HAMSTRING CURLS

6. WALL SIDE LEG LIFTS

7. WALL HIP ABDUCTION

8. WALL HIP HINGE

9. WALL KNEE EXTENSIONS

10. WALL HIP FLEXOR STRETCH

4. BALANCE AND STABILITY EXERCISES

1. WALL BALANCING POSE

Target Muscle Group: This exercise primarily targets the leg muscles, particularly the quadriceps, hamstrings, and glutes, while also engaging the core muscles for stability.

Not Recommended for: Individuals with severe balance issues or recent injuries affecting stability.

INSTRUCTIONS:

1. **Starting Position:**
   Stand with your back to the wall, approximately 6-12 inches away from a wall. Keep your feet hip-width apart, ensuring a firm grounding.

2. **Balance against the Wall:**
   Gently lean backward until your back touches the wall. Let your spine align comfortably against it. Lift one leg off the ground, bending the knee at a 90-degree angle and holding it up in front of you.

3. **Hold & Stabilize:**
   Hold the lifted leg in this position while maintaining a straight posture and engaging your core muscles for balance. Focus your gaze on a fixed point to aid in stability.

4. **Switch Legs:**
   After a few seconds, switch to the other leg and repeat the balancing pose.

5. **Gradual Progress:**
   As comfort and stability improve, attempt to increase the duration of the balancing pose on each leg.

COMPLICATIONS:

1. **For Beginners:** Initial discomfort may arise due to the balancing aspect. Start with short durations and gradually increase the time spent in the pose as balance improves.

2. **For Advanced:** Advanced practitioners can add challenges by closing their eyes while balancing against the wall. They can also extend one leg forward or sideways for an increased balance challenge.

HELPFUL HINT: Use the wall for support and balance; it's crucial to keep a relaxed breathing pattern and avoid holding the breath. Start with short intervals and gradually extend the duration as your stability and balance improve. Focus on engaging the core muscles to stabilize your posture.

2. WALL HEEL RAISES FOR BALANCE

Target Muscle Group: Primarily targets the calf muscles while emphasizing balance and stability.

Not Recommended for: Individuals with severe ankle injuries or recent surgeries affecting the calf muscles or lower limbs.

INSTRUCTIONS:

1. **Starting Position:**
   Stand facing the wall with your feet hip-width apart, a comfortable distance away from the wall.

2. **Engage the Wall:**
   Gently lean forward until your hands touch the wall, maintaining a slight bend in your elbows. Ensure your spine is neutral and your core is engaged.

3. **Heel Raise Movement:**
   Begin by lifting both heels off the ground, rising onto the balls of your feet. Hold the raised position for a moment, feeling the stretch in your calf muscles.

4. **Lowering Phase:**
   Slowly lower your heels back down to the ground, maintaining control and stability. Aim for a smooth, controlled movement throughout the exercise.

5. **Repeat the Motion:**
   Perform several repetitions of the heel raises, focusing on maintaining balance and control with each repetition.

COMPLICATIONS:

1. **For Beginners:** Initial discomfort might arise due to calf engagement. Start with a small range of motion and gradually increase as strength and balance improve.

2. **For Advanced:** To enhance difficulty, perform the raises on a single leg or use a step to deepen the stretch.

HELPFUL HINT: Utilize the wall for support and balance. Maintain a controlled breathing pattern throughout the exercise. Start with a small range of motion and gradually increase the movement as your calf muscles strengthen. Engage your core muscles to stabilize your posture during the exercise.

3. WALL TOE TAPS FOR STABILITY

Target Muscle Group: Primarily engages the lower abdominal muscles while emphasizing balance and stability.

Not Recommended for: Individuals with recent lower abdominal surgeries or severe abdominal strains.

INSTRUCTIONS:

1. **Starting Position:**
Stand facing the wall with your feet hip-width apart, a comfortable distance away from the wall.

2. **Engage the Wall:**
Gently lean forward until your hands touch the wall, maintaining a slight bend in your elbows. Ensure your spine is neutral and your core is engaged.

3. **Toe Tap Movement:**
Lift one foot off the ground, keeping the leg straight. Slowly tap the toe of the lifted foot against the wall, maintaining control and stability. Return the foot to the starting position.

4. **Alternate Legs:**
Perform the same tapping movement with the opposite foot while maintaining balance and control.

5. **Repeat the Motion:**
Alternate tapping between the feet, aiming for a smooth and controlled movement throughout.

COMPLICATIONS:

1. **For Beginners:** Initial discomfort in the lower abdominal region might arise. Start with small movements and gradually increase range and intensity as comfort improves.

2. **For Advanced:** Increase the difficulty by performing the exercise on an unstable surface like a balance pad or by incorporating speed in the tapping motion.

HELPFUL HINT: Utilize the wall for support and balance. Maintain a steady and controlled breathing pattern throughout the exercise. Start with small movements and gradually increase the range and speed of the tapping motion as your lower abdominal strength improves. Focus on engaging the lower abdominal muscles to maintain stability during the exercise.

4. WALL KNEE LIFTS FOR BALANCE

Target Muscle Group: Primarily engages the core muscles, including the lower abdominal and hip flexor muscles, focusing on balance and stability.

Not Recommended for: Individuals with acute hip or knee injuries, recent surgeries on the lower extremities, or those experiencing severe discomfort while lifting the knee.

INSTRUCTIONS:

1. **Starting Position:**
   Stand facing the wall with your feet hip-width apart, a comfortable distance away from the wall.

2. **Engage the Wall:**
   Gently lean forward until your hands touch the wall, maintaining a slight bend in your elbows. Ensure your spine is neutral and your core is engaged.

3. **Knee Lift Movement:**
   Lift one knee towards your chest, aiming to bring it as close to your chest as comfortable. Hold the lifted knee position briefly while maintaining balance and stability. Return the foot to the starting position.

4. **Alternate Legs:**
   Perform the same knee lift movement with the opposite leg while maintaining balance and control.

5. **Repeat the Motion:**
   Alternate lifting between the knees, aiming for a smooth and controlled movement throughout.

COMPLICATIONS:

1. **For Beginners:** Initial discomfort or instability might be felt in the hips or lower back. Start with small movements and gradually increase range and speed as comfort improves.

2. **For Advanced:** Increase difficulty by incorporating variations like holding the lifted knee position for an extended duration or performing the knee lifts with added ankle weights for resistance.

HELPFUL HINT: Utilize the wall for support and balance. Maintain a steady and controlled breathing pattern throughout the exercise. Start with small movements and gradually increase the range and speed of the knee lifts as your lower abdominal and hip flexor strength improves. Focus on engaging the core muscles to maintain stability during the exercise.

5. WALL SIDE LEG RAISES FOR STABILITY

Target Muscle Group: Engages the hip abductor muscles, particularly the outer thighs and hip stabilizers, focusing on balance and stability.

Not Recommended for: Individuals with acute hip, knee, or lower back injuries. Those experiencing discomfort while lifting the leg sideways should avoid this exercise.

INSTRUCTIONS:

1. **Starting Position:**
   Stand upright with your back facing the wall, maintaining a slight distance away.

2. **Hand Support:**
   Place one hand lightly on the wall for balance while keeping your posture tall and your core engaged.

3. **Leg Lift Movement:**
   Slowly lift the outside leg sideways away from the wall, keeping it straight or slightly bent at the knee. Aim to lift the leg to a comfortable height without compromising balance or tilting your upper body. Hold the lifted leg position briefly, focusing on maintaining balance and stability.

4. **Lower the Leg:**
   Gradually lower the leg back to the starting position, maintaining control throughout the movement.

5. **Repeat on Both Sides:**
   Perform the same movement with the opposite leg, focusing on balance and controlled lifting.

COMPLICATIONS:

1. **For Beginners:** Initial instability or discomfort might be felt while lifting the leg sideways. Start with small movements and gradually increase range and speed as comfort improves.

1. **For Advanced:** Enhance the difficulty by holding the lifted leg position for a longer duration or using ankle weights for added resistance.

HELPFUL HINT: Utilize the wall for support and stability. Start with small leg lifts and gradually increase the range of motion as your outer thigh and hip stabilizer muscles strengthen. Focus on maintaining proper posture and engaging the core for balance and stability during the exercise.

6. WALL ONE-LEGGED SQUAT

Target Muscle Group: Engages the quadriceps, glutes, and hamstrings, focusing on balance and lower body stability.

Not Recommended for: Individuals with severe knee issues, recent injuries, or joint instability. Avoid if experiencing acute pain or discomfort during the movement.

INSTRUCTIONS:

1. **Starting Position:**
   Stand upright next to the wall. Ensure your feet are planted firmly on the ground and hip-width apart.

2. **Single Leg Balance:**
   Shift your weight onto one leg, slightly lifting the opposite foot off the ground. Use the wall for support if needed, placing the fingertips lightly against the wall at shoulder height.

3. **Squat Movement:**
   Slowly lower your body into a squat position by bending the supporting knee, keeping the knee aligned with the toes and hips square. Lower your body as far as comfortable or until the thigh is parallel to the floor, maintaining control and balance.

   Ensure the knee of the supporting leg doesn't collapse inward and the back remains straight throughout the movement.

4. **Return to Starting Position:**
   Push through the heel of the supporting leg to rise back to the starting position, maintaining control.

5. **Repeat on Both Legs:**
   Perform the same movement with the opposite leg, focusing on balance and controlled squats.

COMPLICATIONS:

1. **For Beginners:** Initial imbalance or lack of strength might cause difficulty in maintaining stability. Start with partial squats and gradually progress to a deeper squat as strength and balance improve.

2. **For Advanced:** Enhance the difficulty by performing the squats without the wall for support or by incorporating resistance, such as holding weights.

HELPFUL HINT: Use the wall for support and stability, focusing on the movement's quality rather than depth. Begin with partial squats, gradually progressing to deeper squats as strength and balance improve. Maintain proper knee alignment and engage the core for stability throughout the movement.

7. WALL PLANK WITH ALTERNATING LEG LIFTS

Target Muscle Group: Engages the core muscles, glutes, and stabilizer muscles in the legs, emphasizing balance and stability.

Not Recommended for: Individuals with recent injuries or issues affecting their ability to support their weight on their arms or legs. Avoid if experiencing discomfort or pain during the movement.

INSTRUCTIONS:

1. **Starting Position:**
   Stand facing the wall, about an arm's length away. Lean forward and place your palms flat against the wall, slightly lower than shoulder height, creating a straight line from the head to the heels.

2. **Plank Position:**
   Extend your legs backward, resting on the balls of your feet, keeping your body in a straight line, engaging your core muscles.

3. **Alternating Leg Lifts:**
   While maintaining the plank position, lift one foot off the ground a few inches. Hold for a moment, then lower it back down. Alternate between legs, lifting one at a time while keeping the body stable and the hips level.

4. **Maintain Alignment:**
   Focus on keeping the hips level throughout the movement, preventing excessive rotation or sagging of the lower back.

5. **Repeat Leg Lifts:**
   Perform the leg lifts for a set duration or number of repetitions, ensuring stability and control.

COMPLICATIONS:

1. **For Beginners:** Initial difficulty in maintaining balance or supporting body weight on the arms might be experienced. Start with shorter holds and fewer leg lifts, gradually increasing duration and repetitions as strength and balance improve.

2. **For Advanced:** To make the exercise more challenging, extend the duration of the plank hold, increase the number of leg lifts, or introduce additional movements like bringing the lifted leg towards the chest or incorporating a mini hop during leg lifts.

HELPFUL HINT: Start with shorter durations and fewer leg lifts, gradually increasing as strength and stability improve. Maintain a neutral spine and engage the core muscles to support the body throughout the exercise. Focus on controlling the movement and avoid arching the lower back excessively.

8. WALL LATERAL LEG SWING

Target Muscle Group: Engages the abductors, adductors, glutes, and core muscles, promoting balance and stability in the lower body.

Not Recommended for: Individuals with acute knee injuries, hip problems, or instability issues in the lower body. It's crucial to avoid this exercise if experiencing pain or discomfort in the hips, knees, or lower back.

INSTRUCTIONS:

1. **Starting Position:**
   Stand sideways next to a wall, maintaining a slight distance, with one hand lightly resting on the wall for support.

2. **Stance:**
   Ensure a neutral spine, engage your core muscles, and maintain a soft bend in the standing leg.

3. **Leg Swing:**
   Swing the leg farthest from the wall gently across the body, aiming for a controlled lateral movement. Swing the leg back in the opposite direction, extending it to the side while keeping it under control.

4. **Repeat Movement:**
   Perform the swings for a set duration or number of repetitions while maintaining balance and control throughout the movement.

5. **Switch Sides:**
   Perform the same number of swings on the other leg by changing your position and facing the opposite direction.

COMPLICATIONS:

1. **For Beginners:** Initial difficulty in maintaining balance or controlling the swing may occur. It's advised to start with smaller swings and gradually increase the range of motion as balance improves.

2. **For Advanced:** To intensify the exercise, increase the swing's range of motion, perform the swings with ankle weights, or incorporate variations like pulsing at the top of the swing or holding the leg at the highest point for a few seconds.

HELPFUL HINT: Begin with smaller swings and focus on control and balance. Use the wall for light support to maintain stability. Engage the core muscles to stabilize the body throughout the exercise. Gradually increase the range of motion as balance and control improve.

9. WALL STANDING HIP CIRCLES

Target Muscle Group: Engages the hip flexors, abductors, adductors, and core muscles, promoting flexibility and stability in the hips and lower body.

Not Recommended for: Individuals with acute hip injuries, severe hip joint problems, or recent surgeries in the lower body. Avoid if experiencing acute pain or discomfort in the hips, lower back, or pelvis.

INSTRUCTIONS:

1. **Starting Position:**
   Stand facing the wall, maintaining a slight distance, with your feet shoulder-width apart and lightly resting your hands on the wall for support.

2. **Stance:**
   Keep a neutral spine, engage your core muscles, and slightly bend your knees to ease into the movement.

3. **Hip Circles:**
   Begin by slowly rotating your hips in a circular motion, leading with the pelvis. Move the hips to the right, forward, left, and then back to the starting position, forming a circular motion. Gradually increase the size of the circle while maintaining control and balance.

4. **Repeat in Reverse:**
   After completing circles in one direction, switch and perform circles in the opposite direction.

5. **Switch Sides:**
   If desired, repeat the same sequence on the other leg by changing your position and facing the opposite direction.

COMPLICATIONS:

1. **For Beginners:** Initial difficulty in controlling the range of motion or maintaining balance might occur. Start with smaller circles, gradually increasing the range as balance improves.

2. **For Advanced:** To make the exercise more challenging, increase the size of the circles, perform the circles on one leg only, or incorporate ankle weights for added resistance.

HELPFUL HINT: Start with smaller circles and focus on control and balance. Use the wall for light support to maintain stability. Engage the core muscles throughout the movement to stabilize the body. Gradually increase the circle size as balance and control improve.

BALANCE AND STABILITY EXERCISES

1. WALL BALANCING POSE

2. WALL HEEL RAISES FOR BALANCE

3. WALL TOE TAPS FOR STABILITY

4. WALL KNEE LIFTS FOR BALANCE

5. WALL SIDE LEG RAISES FOR STABILITY

6. WALL ONE-LEGGED SQUAT

7. WALL PLANK WITH ALTERNATING LEG LIFTS

8. WALL LATERAL LEG SWING

9. WALL STANDING HIP CIRCLE

5. FLEXIBILITY AND STRETCHING EXERCISES

1. WALL CHEST OPENER STRETCH

Target Muscle Group: Primarily stretches the chest muscles, shoulders, and the front of the shoulders.

Not Recommended for: Individuals with shoulder injuries, severe shoulder impingement, or any recent surgery in the chest or shoulder area. Avoid if you're experiencing acute pain or discomfort in the chest, shoulders, or upper back.

INSTRUCTIONS:

1. **Starting Position:**
Stand sideways next to a wall with feet shoulder-width apart. Place one hand on the wall at shoulder height, with the elbow slightly bent.

2. **Positioning the Body:**
Rotate your body away from the wall while maintaining contact with the hand against the wall. Your torso should be turned away from the wall, and the arm should be in line with the shoulder.

3. **Stretching Movement:**
Slowly rotate your body away from the wall, feeling a gentle stretch across the chest and the front of the shoulder. Maintain a relaxed breathing pattern and avoid pushing into any discomfort or pain. The stretch should feel comfortable and controlled.

4. **Hold and Release:**
Hold the stretched position for 15-30 seconds, feeling the chest muscles elongate. Then, gently release the stretch and return to the starting position.

5. **Repeat on the Other Side:**
Switch sides and repeat the stretch with the opposite arm.

COMPLICATIONS:

1. **For Beginners:** To intensify the stretch, modify the angle of the arm or increase the duration of the stretch by holding the position longer.

2. **For Advanced:** To intensify the stretch, modify the angle of the arm or increase the duration of the stretch by holding the position longer.

HELPFUL HINT: Begin with a mild stretch, focusing on maintaining proper form and feeling a comfortable stretch across the chest. Avoid forcing the stretch; it should be gentle and controlled. Gradually increase the duration and range of the stretch as flexibility improves.

2. WALL CLOCK ARM STRETCH

Target Muscle Group: Primarily stretches the shoulders, deltoids, and upper back muscles.

Not Recommended for: Individuals with recent shoulder injuries, severe shoulder impingement, or limited shoulder mobility. Avoid this exercise if you experience acute pain or discomfort in the shoulders or upper back.

INSTRUCTIONS:

1. **Starting Position:**
   Stand by the wall and lean your shoulder against it. Your feet should be shoulder-width apart and firmly planted on the ground.

2. **Arm Positioning:**
   Extend one arm straight out in front of you at shoulder height and place the palm flat against the wall.

3. **Stretching Movement:**
   Gently rotate your arm while maintaining contact between the hand and the wall. You'll feel a stretch across the front of the shoulder and into the chest as you rotate.

4. **Repeat on the Other Side:**
   Switch arms and repeat the stretch with the opposite arm.

COMPLICATIONS:

1. **For Beginners:** Initial limitations in shoulder flexibility might cause discomfort. Start with smaller movements and gradually increase the stretch as flexibility improves.

2. **For Advanced:** To deepen the stretch, increase the angle of the arm or use a larger range of motion by gradually moving closer to the wall.

HELPFUL HINT: Begin with a mild stretch and focus on maintaining a comfortable, controlled movement. Avoid any sharp or intense pain during the stretch. Gradually increase the stretch's duration and range as your shoulder flexibility improves. Keep the movement smooth and controlled without forcing any uncomfortable positions.

3. WALL UPPER BACK STRETCH

Target Muscle Group: Primarily targets the upper back muscles, including the trapezius and rhomboids.

Not Recommended for: Individuals with existing upper back injuries, recent shoulder dislocations, or severe limitations in upper body mobility. Avoid this exercise if you feel acute pain or discomfort in the upper back or shoulders.

INSTRUCTIONS:

1. **Starting Position:**
   Stand facing the wall, maintaining an arm's length distance. Ensure your feet are planted firmly, shoulder-width apart.

2. **Arm Positioning:**
   Raise both arms straight up and place your palms flat against the wall, slightly higher than shoulder height.

3. **Stretching Movement:**
   Lean your body forward, allowing your chest to approach the wall while keeping your arms extended. Gently press your chest towards the wall, feeling a stretch across the upper back and between the shoulder blades.

4. **Hold and Relax:**
   Hold the stretched position for 15-30 seconds while taking deep breaths. Relax into the stretch without forcing the movement.

5. **Return to Starting Position:**
   Slowly step back from the wall and lower your arms, returning to the standing position.

COMPLICATIONS:

1. **For Beginners:** Initial stiffness or discomfort may be experienced due to limited flexibility in the upper back. Begin with gentle movements, gradually increasing the stretch as comfort allows.

1. **For Advanced:** To deepen the stretch, extend the arms higher on the wall or try variations like adding gentle twists for increased intensity.

HELPFUL HINT: Start with a mild stretch, focusing on maintaining a comfortable position. Breathe deeply throughout the stretch, allowing your body to relax into the movement. Gradually increase the stretch as your upper back flexibility improves. Avoid overextending or pushing into any position that causes discomfort or pain.

4. WALL TRICEP STRETCH

Target Muscle Group: Primarily targets the triceps, the muscles on the back of the upper arm.

Not Recommended for: Individuals with recent shoulder dislocations, acute shoulder injuries, or those with severe limitations in upper body mobility. Avoid this exercise if you experience discomfort or pain in the shoulders or arms during the stretch.

INSTRUCTIONS:

1. **Starting Position:**
   Stand facing the wall, maintaining a comfortable distance from it.
2. **Arm Placement:**
   Raise one arm overhead and bend it at the elbow, bringing the hand towards the upper back. Place the palm of your hand flat against the wall, keeping the elbow pointed upwards.
3. **Stretching Movement:**
   Gently press the palm against the wall while allowing your body to lean slightly forward. Feel the stretch along the back of the upper arm (tricep).
4. **Hold and Breathe:**
   Maintain the stretch for 15-30 seconds, breathing deeply and avoiding any bouncing or sudden movements.
5. **Switch Sides:**
   Release the stretch, switch arms, and repeat the process on the opposite side.

COMPLICATIONS:

1. **For Beginners:** Initial discomfort or tightness might be experienced due to limited tricep flexibility. Start with a mild stretch, gradually increasing the range of motion as comfort allows.
2. **For Advanced:** To deepen the stretch, adjust the position of the arm and hand on the wall. Consider using a resistance band or towel for added leverage to intensify the stretch.

HELPFUL HINT: Begin with a mild stretch, gradually increasing the pressure on the tricep as your flexibility improves. Avoid overextending or pushing into any position that causes discomfort or pain. Breathe deeply throughout the stretch to relax the muscles and enhance the effectiveness of the stretch.

5. WALL SPINAL TWIST STRETCH

Target Muscle Group: Primarily targets the muscles along the spine, particularly the obliques and lower back.

Not Recommended for: Individuals with recent spinal injuries, herniated discs, or severe limitations in spinal mobility. Avoid this exercise if you experience acute pain, discomfort, or strain during the twist.

INSTRUCTIONS:

1. **Starting Position:**
Stand upright with your back facing the wall, maintaining a comfortable distance from it.

2. **Feet and Hip Placement:**
Keep your feet positioned hip-width apart and flat on the ground. Engage your core by gently pulling your navel inwards towards your spine.

3. **Twisting Movement:**
Slowly place one hand on the wall at shoulder height, keeping the arm straight. Rotate your torso away from the wall, twisting gently through the waist, and look over the opposite shoulder. Allow the twist to come from the midsection of your body rather than forcing the movement from your arms or shoulders.

4. **Hold and Breathe:**
Maintain the twist for 15-30 seconds, focusing on deep breaths to encourage relaxation and increased flexibility.

5. **Switch Sides:**
Release the twist, switch arms, and repeat the process on the opposite side.

COMPLICATIONS:

1. **For Beginners:** Beginners may find it challenging to balance during the stretch or experience difficulty in bringing the heel closer to the buttocks. Begin with a mild stretch and gradually increase the intensity.

2. **For Advanced:** Advanced practitioners can deepen the stretch by enhancing the position. They can hold the foot farther up towards the buttocks or use props like a yoga strap to pull the foot closer to intensify the stretch.

HELPFUL HINT: Initiate the twist gradually, respecting your body's limitations. Avoid over-twisting or pushing into any position that causes discomfort. Focus on controlled breathing and a gentle twist to enhance spinal flexibility without strain.

6. WALL HAMSTRING STRETCH

Target Muscle Group: Hamstrings

Not Recommended for: Individuals with acute hamstring injuries or those with limited range of motion in the hips and knees.

INSTRUCTIONS:

1. **Starting Position:**
   Lie on your back with your buttocks close to a wall, legs extended upward, and resting against the wall. Ensure your spine is aligned and relaxed, with your arms resting comfortably by your sides.

2. **Leg Positioning:**
   Raise both legs up the wall, keeping them straight and in line with your hips. Bend one leg at the knee as much as possible, bringing the foot towards your buttocks, while keeping the other leg straight against the wall.

3. **Stretching:**
   With the bent leg, gently pull the knee towards your chest, feeling a stretch along the back of the thigh and hamstring. Hold this position for 20-30 seconds, breathing deeply and relaxing into the stretch.

4. **Release and Switch:**
   Slowly release the bent leg and return it to the starting position against the wall. Switch legs, bending the opposite leg at the knee and repeating the stretch on the other side.

5. **Repeat:**
   Perform 2-3 sets of stretches on each leg, gradually increasing the duration of the stretch as you feel more comfortable.

COMPLICATIONS:

1. **For Beginners:** Start with a gentle stretch, avoiding overstretching or pushing beyond your comfort level. Focus on maintaining proper alignment and breathing throughout the exercise.

2. **For Advanced:** Advanced practitioners may deepen the stretch by straightening the bent leg further or by placing a towel or resistance band around the foot of the extended leg to increase the intensity of the stretch.

HELPFUL HINT: Pay attention to any sensations of discomfort or pain during the stretch, and avoid pushing beyond your limits. Focus on maintaining a gentle, consistent stretch and breathe deeply to promote relaxation and flexibility.

7. WALL QUADRICEPS STRETCH

Target Muscle Group: Primarily targets the quadriceps muscles at the front of the thigh.

Not Recommended for: Individuals with acute knee injuries, recent knee surgeries, or chronic knee issues. Avoid this exercise if you experience acute pain or discomfort in the knees during the stretch.

INSTRUCTIONS:

1. **Starting Position:**
   Stand facing the wall at an arm's length away. Maintain an erect posture with your feet hip-width apart.

2. **Execution:**
   Reach back and place one hand against the wall for balance. Bend one knee, bringing your heel towards your buttocks, and grab the ankle or foot with the hand on the same side. Ensure the knees stay close together and avoid overarching the lower back.

3. **Stretch Movement:**
   Gently pull the heel towards the buttocks, feeling a stretch in the front of the thigh. Keep the body upright and avoid leaning forward excessively.

4. **Hold and Breathe:**
   Hold the stretch for 30 seconds to 1 minute, focusing on steady breathing to relax into the stretch.

5. **Switch Sides:**
   Release the stretch, switch legs, and repeat the process on the opposite leg.

COMPLICATIONS:

1. **For Beginners:** Initial stiffness or discomfort may be experienced due to limited flexibility in the upper back. Begin with gentle movements, gradually increasing the stretch as comfort allows.

1. **For Advanced:** To deepen the stretch, extend the arms higher on the wall or try variations like adding gentle twists for increased intensity.

HELPFUL HINT: Maintain a stable and controlled position throughout the stretch. Avoid overarching the lower back or leaning forward excessively. Gradually increase the intensity of the stretch over time without causing discomfort or pain in the knees. Focus on breathing deeply to encourage relaxation and increased flexibility in the quadriceps.

8. WALL CALF STRETCH

Target Muscle Group: Primarily targets the calf muscles located at the back of the lower leg.

Not Recommended for: Individuals with Achilles tendon injuries, severe ankle issues, or those experiencing acute pain in the calves or ankles.

INSTRUCTIONS:

1. **Starting Position:**
   Stand facing the wall at an arm's length, placing both hands against the wall at shoulder height for support.

2. **Execution:**
   Take a step back with one foot and keep it flat on the ground. Extend the other leg straight behind you, placing the ball of your foot against the wall, ensuring the heel is on or close to the ground.

3. **Stretch Movement:**
   Lean forward, shifting your hips slightly towards the wall, until you feel a stretch in the calf of the extended leg.

4. **Hold and Breathe:**
   Hold the stretch for 30 seconds to 1 minute, breathing deeply and allowing the calf muscles to relax into the stretch.

5. **Switch Sides:**
   Release the stretch, switch legs, and repeat the process with the opposite leg.

COMPLICATIONS:

1. **For Beginners:** Beginners might struggle to maintain balance or feel discomfort in the calf muscles during the stretch. Start with a mild stretch and gradually increase the intensity.

2. **For Advanced:** To intensify, individuals can try placing the foot slightly higher on the wall or use props like a folded towel or yoga block under the ball of the foot to increase the stretch.

HELPFUL HINT: Maintain a stable and controlled position during the stretch. Ensure the heel stays grounded to maximize the calf stretch. Avoid bouncing or overstretching the calf muscles. Gradually increase the intensity of the stretch over time without causing discomfort. Focus on breathing deeply to encourage relaxation and increased flexibility in the calf muscles.

9. WALL HIP FLEXOR STRETCH

Target Muscle Group: Primarily targets the hip flexors, located in the front of the hip.

Not Recommended for: Individuals with acute hip or lower back injuries. Avoid this stretch if it causes discomfort or exacerbates existing pain.

INSTRUCTIONS:

1. **Starting Position:**
   Stand facing by the wall, approximately an arm's length away. Place your hands on the wall at shoulder height for support.

2. **Execution:**
   Take a step back with one foot, keeping the other foot planted firmly on the ground in front of you. Bend the front knee slightly and press the back heel down toward the floor.

3. **Stretch Movement:**
   Keep your torso upright and gently lean forward, shifting your hips slightly forward until you feel a stretch in the front of the back leg's hip. Ensure the back heel remains on the ground and the front knee is aligned over the ankle.

4. **Hold and Breathe:**
   Hold the stretch for 30 seconds to 1 minute while maintaining steady breathing.

5. **Switch Sides:**
   Release the stretch, switch legs, and repeat the process with the opposite leg.

COMPLICATIONS:

1. **For Beginners:** Beginners might find it challenging to maintain balance during the stretch. Start with a gentle stretch and gradually increase the intensity.

2. **For Advanced:** Advanced individuals can increase the stretch by stepping the forward leg farther from the wall or incorporating a gentle pelvic tilt forward to deepen the hip flexor stretch.

HELPFUL HINT: Focus on maintaining a stable posture throughout the stretch. Avoid overarching the lower back or leaning too far forward to prevent strain. Concentrate on breathing deeply and relaxing into the stretch. Gradually increase the depth of the stretch over time without causing discomfort.

10. WALL GLUTE STRETCH

Target Muscle Group: Primarily targets the glutes (buttocks) and may also engage the hips and lower back.

Not Recommended for: Individuals with severe hip injuries or acute lower back pain. Avoid this stretch if it causes sharp pain or discomfort.

 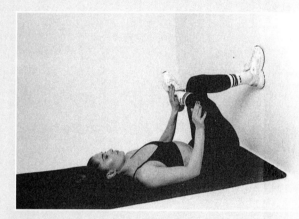

INSTRUCTIONS:

1. **Starting Position:**
Lie on your back on the floor, raise your legs up on the wall.

2. **Execution:**
Lift your right leg and cross it over your left thigh, creating a figure-four shape. Bend your left knee slightly and lower your hips down toward the wall until you feel a comfortable stretch in the outer part of your right glute.

3. **Stretch Movement:**
Gently press your right knee towards the wall while keeping your back straight and your chest lifted. Hold the stretch and feel the gentle release in the glute muscles.

4. **Hold and Breathe:**
Hold the position for about 30 seconds to 1 minute, maintaining regular breathing.

5. **Switch Sides:**
Release the stretch, uncross your leg, and switch to the other side, repeating the stretch with the left leg crossed over the right thigh.

COMPLICATIONS:

1. **For Beginners:** Beginners might find it challenging to balance and maintain the stretch. Start with a mild stretch and gradually increase the intensity.

2. **For Advanced:** To deepen the stretch, consider performing a seated or lying glute stretch, incorporating variations like twisting the torso or adding resistance bands for extra tension.

HELPFUL HINT: Ensure your movements are slow and controlled. Focus on maintaining good posture and avoid rounding your back. Gradually deepen the stretch over time without forcing it. If balance is challenging, perform this stretch near a sturdy object for added support.

FLEXIBILITY AND STRETCHING EXERCISES

1. WALL CHEST OPENER STRETCH

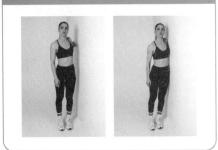

2. WALL CLOCK ARM STRETCH

3. WALL UPPER BACK STRETCH

4. WALL TRICEP STRETCH

5. WALL SPINAL TWIST STRETCH

6. WALL HAMSTRING STRETCH

7. WALL QUADRICEPS STRETCH

8. WALL CALF STRETCH

9. WALL HIP FLEXOR STRETCH

10. WALL GLUTE STRETCH

6. WHOLE BODY INTEGRATION EXERCISES
1. WALL ROLL DOWN

Target Muscle Group: Engages various muscle groups including the core, hamstrings, back, and shoulders.

Not Recommended for: Individuals with acute back injuries, severe osteoporosis, or those unable to stand comfortably.

INSTRUCTIONS:

1. **Starting Position:**
   Stand with your back against the wall, feet hip-width apart. Keep the spine neutral and engage the core.

2. **Execution:**
   Inhale deeply. As you exhale, begin to articulate your spine sequentially, starting with the chin tucking towards the chest.

   Slowly roll down, segmenting the movement through each vertebra, aiming to touch the wall with each vertebra possible while keeping the arms relaxed.

3. **Stretch Movement:**
   Once your spine is fully rolled down, take a moment to feel the stretch through the back of your legs and maintain a gentle engagement in the core. Hold this position briefly to experience the stretch without strain.

4. **Roll Up:**
   Inhale and begin the return movement by slowly stacking your vertebrae back up against the wall, lifting the head last, maintaining control throughout.

5. **Return to Starting Position:**
   Finish in the neutral starting position with the spine in alignment.

6. **Repetitions:**
   Aim for 5 reps to start, focusing on quality over quantity.

COMPLICATIONS:

1. **For Beginners:** Beginners might find it challenging to maintain proper spinal alignment during the roll down. Start with smaller movements and gradually increase the range of motion.

2. **For Advanced:** To elevate the difficulty, consider performing the exercise on one leg, incorporating resistance bands, or using a Swiss ball against the wall for added instability.

HELPFUL HINT: Keep the movement slow and controlled, focusing on articulating the spine and maintaining a smooth, continuous motion. Avoid any discomfort or pain during the exercise. If needed, perform this exercise under supervision to ensure proper form and technique.

2. WALL CAT-COW STRETCH

Target Muscle Group: Engages the entire spine, core, and shoulder girdle.

Not Recommended for: Individuals with severe neck injuries, spinal issues, or those unable to stand comfortably.

INSTRUCTIONS:

1. **Starting Position:**
   Stand facing the wall, about an arm's length away. Keep the feet hip-width apart, and gently press the palms against the wall at shoulder height.

2. **Cat Position:**
   As you exhale, round the spine away from the wall, drawing the navel toward the spine, tucking the chin toward the chest, and pressing firmly through the hands to create a C-curve in the spine. Feel the stretch through the back and bring awareness to each vertebra's movement.

3. **Cow Position:**
   Inhale deeply and start to arch the spine, allowing the belly to drop toward the wall while lifting the chest and the sit bones. Slightly draw the shoulder blades together, broadening across the collarbones, without collapsing into the lower back.

4. **Flowing Movement:**
   Move slowly and mindfully between the Cat and Cow positions, synchronizing the breath with the movement. Exhale as you transition into Cat, inhale as you transition into Cow, maintaining a smooth, controlled motion.

5. **Repetition:**
   Repeat the Cat-Cow movement for several breath cycles, allowing the spine to gently articulate and the muscles to relax and lengthen.

6. **Conclusion:**
   Finish the sequence with a neutral spine, standing comfortably and relaxed.

COMPLICATIONS:

1. **For Beginners:** Beginners might find it challenging to coordinate the breath with the movement. Start with smaller movements and focus on the quality of the stretch.

2. **For Advanced:** To make it more challenging, consider holding each position for a longer duration, incorporating resistance bands for added tension, or gradually increasing the range of motion.

HELPFUL HINT: Focus on the coordination of breath and movement, allowing the breath to guide the pace. Ensure your shoulders and neck remain relaxed throughout the exercise. It's essential to honor your body's limits and not force any movement that causes discomfort.

3. WALL SPINAL ARTICULATION

Target Muscle Group: Engages and mobilizes the entire spine, enhancing flexibility and core activation.

Not Recommended for: Individuals with severe spinal injuries, acute back pain, or those unable to stand comfortably.

INSTRUCTIONS:

1. **Starting Position:**
Stand with your back against the wall, about an arm's length away. Ensure your feet are hip-width apart, and your back is gently pressed against the wall.

2. **Neutral Spine Position:**
Inhale deeply, lengthening through the crown of the head and allowing the spine to remain in a neutral position. Engage your core by gently pulling the navel towards the spine without excessively arching or flattening the lower back against the wall.

3. **Articulation of the Spine:**
Exhale and start to round the spine, beginning from the tailbone and moving upward vertebra by vertebra. Imagine each vertebra peeling off the wall, creating a C-curve with the spine.

4. **Reverse Movement:**
Inhale at the bottom of the movement, maintaining the rounded position. Start to articulate the spine back up the wall, starting from the lower back and moving towards the neck, vertebra by vertebra.

5. **Flowing Motion:**
Release the stretch, switch legs, and repeat the process with the opposite leg.

6. **Conclusion:**
Return to the neutral spine position, standing comfortably and relaxed against the wall.

COMPLICATIONS:

1. **For Beginners:** Beginners may struggle with the coordination of movement throughout the spine. Start with smaller movements and focus on gradual progression.

2. **For Advanced:** To make it more challenging, consider incorporating resistance bands, increasing the range of motion, or maintaining specific positions for an extended duration.

HELPFUL HINT: Concentrate on the sensation of each vertebra moving and avoid rushing through the exercise. Maintain a consistent breathing pattern and engage your core throughout the movement. Emphasize quality over quantity, ensuring each articulation is controlled and deliberate.

4. WALL PELVIC TILTS

Target Muscle Group: Engages the core muscles, enhancing pelvic mobility and stability.

Not Recommended for: Individuals with acute pelvic pain, pelvic floor dysfunction, or recent pelvic surgeries.

INSTRUCTIONS:

1. **Starting Position:**
   Stand with your back against the wall. Ensure your feet are hip-width apart and positioned comfortably away from the wall. Keep the spine neutral, with the lower back gently touching the wall.

2. **Engage the Core:**
   Inhale deeply, expanding your ribcage without arching the lower back excessively. Engage your abdominal muscles by gently drawing your navel toward your spine.

3. **Pelvic Tilt - Forward and Backward:**
   Exhale and tilt your pelvis forward, creating a small gap between the lower back and the wall. Inhale and tilt your pelvis backward, gently pressing the lower back into the wall. Focus on the movement initiating from the pelvis while keeping the upper body relaxed.

4. **Controlled Movements:**
   Perform the tilting motion with control, avoiding excessive arching or tucking of the pelvis. Continue the sequence, alternating between forward and backward tilts, maintaining a slow and controlled pace.

5. **Repeat and Flow:**
   Aim for smooth transitions between the forward and backward tilts, ensuring a continuous and controlled flow of movement. Keep the breath steady and coordinated with the pelvic movements.

6. **Conclusion:**
   Gradually return to the neutral pelvic position, keeping the lower back gently against the wall.

COMPLICATIONS:

1. **For Beginners:** Initially, beginners may struggle with isolating pelvic movements. Focus on small tilts to avoid overexertion.

2. **For Advanced:** To heighten difficulty, consider performing the exercise on an unstable surface or incorporating resistance bands.

HELPFUL HINT: Maintain a relaxed upper body and focus on isolating the pelvic movements. Keep the tilts small and controlled, prioritizing precision over the range of motion. Engage the core throughout the exercise to stabilize the pelvis.

5. WALL FULL-BODY CIRCLES

Target Muscle Group: Engages the core, enhances spinal mobility, and encourages full-body coordination.

Not Recommended for: Individuals with severe joint issues or those who experience dizziness or instability when standing for extended periods.

INSTRUCTIONS:

1. **Starting Position:**
Stand facing the wall, maintaining a comfortable distance away from it. Position yourself with your feet shoulder-width apart, ensuring a grounded stance. Keep your arms extended.

2. **Engage the Core:**
Activate your core by gently pulling your navel toward your spine, maintaining a neutral spine position.

3. **Circular Movement:**
Start by initiating a slow and controlled circular movement through your body. Move the body in a circular pattern, starting from the head, then shoulders, torso, hips, and down to the legs while maintaining contact with the wall.

Circle back up from the legs to the hips, torso, shoulders, and head in a fluid and controlled motion. Ensure the movement is seamless, focusing on a continuous flow without jerks or pauses.

4. **Repeat and Alternate Directions:**
Perform the circular motion in one direction for several repetitions, maintaining a steady rhythm. After completing repetitions in one direction, switch and perform the circles in the opposite direction for balance.

5. **Controlled Breathing:**
Coordinate the circular movement with controlled breathing. Inhale deeply as you ascend, and exhale slowly as you descend.

6. **Conclusion:**
Gradually slow down the movement and return to the initial standing position.

COMPLICATIONS:

1. **For Beginners:** Beginners might initially struggle with coordinating the circular movement. Start with smaller circles and gradually increase the range of motion.

2. **For Advanced:** To intensify, consider increasing the number of repetitions, incorporating resistance bands, or performing the circles at a slower pace to challenge stability.

HELPFUL HINT: Start with smaller circles and gradually increase the size and range of motion as you become more comfortable. Maintain a stable stance and focus on the fluidity of the movement, engaging the core throughout. Be mindful of your breathing pattern and avoid any sudden or jerky movements.

6. WALL SQUAT TO OVERHEAD REACH

Target Muscle Group: Engages the lower body, core, and upper extremities while promoting overall stability and mobility.

Not Recommended for: Individuals with severe knee or hip issues or those who have difficulty maintaining a squat position against a wall.

INSTRUCTIONS:

1. **Starting Position:**
   Stand by the wall, about two feet away, with feet slightly wider than hip-width apart. Lean against the wall, ensuring your back is flat against it, and your feet are firmly planted on the ground. Engage your core by gently drawing your navel towards your spine.

2. **Squat Movement:**
   Lower your body into a squat position, bending your knees and hips while sliding down the wall. Aim to descend until your thighs are parallel to the ground, ensuring your knees stay aligned with your toes.

3. **Overhead Reach:**
   From the squat position, maintain stability and extend your arms alternatively overhead, reaching toward the ceiling. Focus on a controlled movement without arching your lower back excessively.

4. **Return to Starting Position:**
   Lower your arms back down to shoulder height while simultaneously rising from the squat by pushing through your heels. Straighten your legs gradually, returning to the initial standing position with control.

5. **Repetition:**
   Repeat the squat-to-reach motion in a fluid and controlled manner for several repetitions.

6. **Breathing Pattern:**
   Inhale as you lower into the squat position and exhale as you rise and reach overhead.

COMPLICATIONS:

1. **For Beginners:** Initial difficulty might arise in maintaining a correct squat form. Begin with shallow squats and gradually progress to a deeper squat as comfort and strength improve.

2. **For Advanced:** To heighten the challenge, incorporate a hold at the lowest point of the squat or add resistance by using light hand weights during the overhead reach.

HELPFUL HINT: Ensure your knees stay aligned with your toes throughout the squat movement. Focus on maintaining a neutral spine and avoid overarching your lower back during the overhead reach. Start with shallow squats and gradually increase depth as your comfort and strength improve.

7. WALL STANDING TWIST

Target Muscle Group: Engages the core muscles, including the obliques and abdominals, while promoting spinal mobility and flexibility.

Not Recommended for: Individuals with severe spinal issues, recent injuries, or those experiencing acute pain in the back or neck.

INSTRUCTIONS:

1. **Starting Position:**
   Stand by the wall, maintaining a distance of about an arm's length away. Keep your feet planted firmly on the ground, about hip-width apart. Extend your arms straight in front of you at shoulder height.

2. **Execution:**
   Engage your core muscles by gently pulling your navel toward your spine. Exhale and rotate your torso to one side, maintaining contact between your palms and the wall. Keep your hips facing forward and avoid twisting at the knees.

3. **Twisting Movement:**
   Hold the twist for a few seconds, feeling the stretch across the torso. Inhale as you return to the center, realigning your spine. Repeat the twist on the opposite side, maintaining control throughout the movement.

4. **Repetition:**
   Alternate between both sides, performing controlled twists for several repetitions or as comfortable.

5. **Breathing Pattern:**
   Exhale as you twist to the side, inhale as you return to the center.

COMPLICATIONS:

1. **For Beginners:** Initially, individuals might find it challenging to maintain balance and stability during the twisting movement. Start with gentle twists and gradually increase the range of motion as comfort and stability improve.

2. **For Advanced:** To enhance the difficulty, increase the speed of the twists, incorporate resistance bands or hand weights, or perform the exercise while balancing on one leg.

HELPFUL HINT: Focus on the rotation originating from the core while maintaining stability through the hips and legs. Start with gentle and controlled movements, gradually increasing the range of motion as flexibility zimproves. Avoid forcing the twist and prioritize maintaining proper alignment to prevent strain on the spine.

8. WALL MODIFIED DOWNWARD DOG

Target Muscle Group: Engages the entire body with emphasis on stretching the hamstrings, calves, shoulders, and lengthening the spine.

Not Recommended for: Individuals with severe shoulder issues, recent injuries, or those experiencing acute pain or discomfort in the neck, shoulders, or lower back.

INSTRUCTIONS:

1. **Starting Position:**
   Stand facing the wall, arms-length away, with your feet hip-width apart. Place your palms flat against the wall at shoulder height, fingers spread comfortably. Walk your hands down the wall as you step back, tilting your pelvis up and straightening your arms.

2. **Execution:**
   Begin by pressing your palms firmly into the wall, ensuring your arms are straight. Walk your feet back until your body forms an inverted "V" shape, keeping your heels on the ground. Maintain a slight bend in the knees if necessary, focusing on lengthening the spine and keeping the head aligned between the arms.

3. **Stretching Movement:**
   Press through your palms and try to straighten your legs, aiming to bring your torso closer to parallel with the ground. Engage your core, and let your head hang between your arms, relaxing your neck and shoulders.

4. **Hold and Breathe:**
   Hold the position for several breaths, feeling the stretch in the hamstrings and shoulders. Keep the breaths deep and controlled.

5. **Release:**
   To come out of the position, gently walk your hands back up the wall and step closer.

COMPLICATIONS:

1. **For Beginners:** Initially, individuals may feel tightness in the hamstrings and shoulders. Start with a gentle stretch, keeping the knees slightly bent if needed, and gradually work towards straightening the legs.

2. **For Advanced:** To increase the challenge, try moving the feet further from the wall, aiming for a deeper stretch. Alternatively, lift one leg at a time to intensify the stretch on the opposite leg and enhance balance.

HELPFUL HINT: Focus on maintaining length in the spine and keeping the weight evenly distributed between the hands and feet. Avoid locking the knees and over-straining the shoulders or hamstrings. Modify the distance from the wall to suit your comfort level and gradually work towards a deeper stretch.

9. WALL ARM-LEG EXTENSION

Target Muscle Group: Engages the core, shoulders, and glutes while enhancing balance and stability.

Not Recommended for: Individuals with recent shoulder or hip injuries, severe balance issues, or those experiencing acute pain or discomfort in the back, shoulders, or hips.

INSTRUCTIONS:

1. **Starting Position:**
   Stand facing the wall, about an arm's length away, with your feet shoulder-width apart. Gently lean forward and place your palms flat against the wall at shoulder height, fingers spread comfortably.

2. **Execution:**
   Engage your core muscles by pulling your navel towards your spine. Simultaneously lift your right leg straight back and your left arm forward, maintaining a parallel line to the ground. Focus on keeping your hips level and avoiding arching your lower back.

3. **Extension Movement:**
   Hold the extended position briefly, ensuring stability and alignment, with your body forming a straight line from the fingertips to the toes. Feel the engagement in your core muscles to maintain balance.

4. **Alternate Sides:**
   Lower your arm and leg back down to the starting position. Repeat the movement, alternating between extending the left arm with the right leg and the right arm with the left leg.

5. **Repetition and Breathing:**
   Perform the exercise for the desired number of repetitions, coordinating your breath with each movement.

COMPLICATIONS:

1. **For Beginners:** Initially, maintaining balance may be challenging. Start by focusing on stability; perform the movement slowly and pause briefly at the extended position.

2. **For Advanced:** To make it more challenging, increase the duration of holding the extended position, or try the exercise on one leg or one arm only for added balance and core engagement.

HELPFUL HINT: Focus on maintaining a neutral spine and engaging your core throughout the movement. Avoid overarching your lower back or rounding your shoulders. Start with small movements and gradually increase the range of motion as you build strength and stability.

10. WALL SIDE BEND

Target Muscle Group: Engages the obliques, lateral core, and stretches the side body muscles.

Not Recommended for: Individuals with recent rib, shoulder, or hip injuries, severe balance issues, or those experiencing acute pain or discomfort in the side body, back, or hips.

INSTRUCTIONS:

1. **Starting Position:**
   Stand sideways with your right side facing the wall, about an arm's length away. Feet are hip-width apart. Extend your right arm overhead, placing the palm flat against the wall. Keep the left arm relaxed by your side.

2. **Execution:**
   Engage your core muscles by gently pulling your navel towards your spine. Inhale deeply and, as you exhale, slowly bend your upper body towards the left, creating a lateral bend along the right side. Keep your hips squared and avoid arching or rounding your lower back.

3. **Bending Movement:**
   Feel the stretch along the right side of your body, from the fingertips down to the hip. Hold the stretch for a few breaths, maintaining a comfortable stretch without overreaching or causing strain.

4. **Return to Starting Position:**
   Inhale and gradually return to the upright position, realigning your body to the starting position against the wall. Relax and switch sides to perform the same movement on the opposite side.

5. **Repetition and Breathing:**
   Repeat the exercise for the desired number of repetitions, coordinating your breath with each movement.

COMPLICATIONS:

1. **For Beginners:** Initially, maintaining balance and achieving the full range of motion might be challenging. Focus on controlled movements and avoiding overreaching to prevent strains.

2. **For Advanced:** To increase difficulty, try extending the hold at the bent position, incorporating a slight twist, or using a resistance band for added tension.

HELPFUL HINT: Focus on maintaining a neutral spine and engaging the core while performing the side bend. Avoid overstretching or leaning too far to prevent strain. Start with smaller movements and gradually increase the range of motion as you build flexibility and control in the lateral core muscles.

WHOLE BODY INTEGRATION EXERCISES

1. WALL ROLL DOWN

2. WALL CAT-COW STRETCH

3. WALL SPINAL ARTICULATION

4. WALL PELVIC TILTS

5. WALL FULL-BODY CIRCLES

6. WALL SQUAT TO OVERHEAD REACH

7. WALL STANDING TWIST

8. WALL MODIFIED DOWNWARD DOG

9. WALL ARM-LEG EXTENSION

10. WALL SIDE BEND

CHAPTER 3. TRACKING PROGRESS AND ADVANCING IN WALL PILATES

Tracking Progress in Wall Pilates

Tracking progress is crucial in a Pilates journey, offering insights into improvements, motivating continued practice, and aiding in setting achievable goals. There are various methods beyond measurements and journaling that can effectively track progress.

1. Measurements and Observations

Body Measurements:
- **Purpose:** Tracking physical changes
- **How-to:** Record measurements of waist, hips, thighs, and arms. Check periodically to note changes in muscle tone or size.

Before-and-After Photos:
- **Purpose:** Visual progress tracking
- **How-to:** Take front, side, and back photos before starting Pilates and periodically thereafter. Compare to observe changes in posture, muscle definition, and body shape.

2. Journaling and Reflective Practices

Exercise Logs:
- **Purpose:** Tracking workout details
- **How-to:** Maintain a workout log detailing exercises performed, repetitions, sets, modifications, and how the body feels post-exercise.

Mindfulness Journaling:
- **Purpose:** Mental and emotional progress tracking
- **How-to:** Record feelings, energy levels, stress levels, and any emotional shifts before and after Pilates sessions to observe mental well-being improvements.

3. Performance-Based Tracking

Progression of Exercises:
- **Purpose:** Monitoring strength and flexibility gains
- **How-to:** Track improvements in executing Pilates exercises. Note increased reps, enhanced form, or the ability to perform advanced variations.

Endurance and Stamina:
- **Purpose:** Tracking physical endurance
- **How-to:** Note changes in the duration of holding positions or sustaining exercises. Observe if it becomes easier to maintain positions over time.

4. Feedback and Self-Assessment

Self-Assessment:
- **Purpose:** Personal reflection and assessment
- **How-to:** Periodically self-assess Pilates practice, noting improvements, challenges, and areas needing more focus. Set realistic goals based on observations.

Instructor or Peer Feedback:
- **Purpose:** External perspective and guidance

- **How-to:** Seek feedback from instructors or peers regarding form, progression, and areas of improvement during practice sessions.

Effective progress tracking in Wall Pilates involves a combination of methods beyond just measurements and journaling. By adopting a holistic approach that includes observations, reflective practices, performance-based monitoring, and seeking feedback, beginners can comprehensively track their progress, celebrate achievements, and make informed adjustments to their practice.

Advancing in Wall Pilates: Strategies and Goal Setting

As beginners progress in Wall Pilates, it's essential to evolve workouts, challenge the body, and set new goals to maintain momentum and growth. Here are strategies for advancing workouts and setting progressive goals.

1. Gradual Intensification

Progressive Resistance:
- **Strategy:** Increase resistance gradually by using resistance bands or Pilates balls to add challenge to exercises.
- **Goal Setting:** Aim to use a higher resistance level or add an extra set/repetition progressively.

Extended Hold Times:
- **Strategy:** Extend the duration of holding positions or exercises against the wall.
- **Goal Setting:** Increase hold times by 5-10 seconds for each exercise or pose.

2. Variation and Complexity

Advanced Exercise Variations:
- **Strategy:** Explore more complex variations of familiar exercises.
- **Goal Setting:** Learn and incorporate advanced variations, such as adding twists or combining movements for added difficulty.

Multi-Planar Movements:
- **Strategy:** Introduce movements in different planes (frontal, sagittal, transverse).
- **Goal Setting:** Include exercises that challenge lateral or rotational movements to enhance overall body control and stability.

3. Focus on Specific Goals

Targeted Muscle Engagement:
- **Strategy:** Focus on isolating specific muscle groups during exercises.
- **Goal Setting:** Develop goals to strengthen particular muscle groups (e.g., core, glutes, shoulders) and measure progress over time.

Improving Flexibility and Range of Motion:
- **Strategy:** Emphasize stretching and flexibility exercises.
- **Goal Setting:** Set goals to improve flexibility in specific areas and measure progress by reaching for greater ranges of motion.

4. Mind-Body Connection and Precision

Refinement of Technique:
- **Strategy:** Concentrate on precision and form during exercises.
- **Goal Setting:** Strive for improved alignment and execution of movements, focusing on controlled and precise actions.

Mindfulness and Breath Awareness:
- **Strategy:** Incorporate breathwork and mindful practices during sessions.
- **Goal Setting:** Work towards deeper breath control, syncing breath with movements for enhanced focus and relaxation.

Advancing in Wall Pilates involves a progressive approach, embracing varied strategies to intensify workouts and setting new, specific goals. By gradually intensifying exercises, exploring variations, focusing on specific goals, and refining technique and mind-body connection, beginners can continually evolve their practice, fostering growth and accomplishment in their Pilates journey.

Cultivating a Mindset of Continual Improvement and Adaptability

In the practice of Wall Pilates, fostering a mindset centered on continual improvement and adaptability is key to sustaining progress and achieving long-term success. Embracing these principles empowers beginners to evolve their practice and navigate their Pilates journey more effectively.

1. Embrace the Journey

Shift from Perfection to Progress:
- **Mindset Shift:** Emphasize progress over perfection. Recognize and celebrate small improvements as milestones on your journey.

Learn from Setbacks:
- **Adaptability Principle:** View setbacks as opportunities for learning and growth rather than failures. Use them as stepping stones for improvement.

2. Openness to Learning

Curiosity and Exploration:
- **Mindset Outlook:** Foster curiosity in exploring new exercises, techniques, and variations. Stay open to learning and discovering different aspects of Pilates.

Seek Guidance and Feedback:
- **Adaptability Practice:** Embrace the guidance of instructors or peers. Welcome feedback to refine techniques and further your understanding.

3. Flexibility in Practice

Adapt to Body Changes:
- **Mindset Perspective:** Acknowledge that the body changes over time. Adapt exercises to accommodate any physical changes or limitations.

Modify and Progress Gradually:
- **Adaptability Approach:** Be willing to modify exercises to suit individual needs. Progress gradually, respecting the body's pace and capabilities.

4. Persistence and Resilience

Consistency in Practice:
- **Mindset Commitment:** Prioritize consistency in practice over occasional intensity. Establishing a routine aids in gradual improvement.

Resilience through Challenges:
- **Adaptability Mindset:** Approach challenges as opportunities for growth. Cultivate resilience by persisting through difficulties encountered in exercises or progress.

A mindset of continual improvement and adaptability in Wall Pilates involves embracing progress, openness to learning, flexibility in practice, and persistence through challenges. By nurturing these principles, beginners can forge a more resilient and adaptable approach to their Pilates journey, enabling sustainable growth and enjoyment in their practice.

MOTIVATION TIPS FOR THRIVING IN WALL PILATES

Maintaining motivation is essential in sustaining a consistent Wall Pilates practice. These tips aim to inspire beginners, ensuring they stay engaged, excited, and committed to their Pilates journey.

1. Define Personal Why

Discover Your Purpose:
- **Tip:** Reflect on why you started Pilates. Is it for strength, flexibility, stress relief, or overall well-being? Understanding your motivation creates a stronger connection to your practice.

Set Meaningful Goals:
- **Tip:** Establish realistic and specific goals. Whether it's mastering a certain exercise, improving flexibility, or enhancing core strength, clear objectives keep you focused.

2. Cultivate a Supportive Environment

Community Engagement:
- **Tip:** Join Pilates groups or forums to connect with like-minded individuals. Sharing experiences and progress with others can boost motivation.

Accountability Partnerships:
- **Tip:** Partner with a friend or family member for accountability. Sharing goals and progress with someone creates mutual encouragement.

3. Diversify and Explore

Variety in Practice:
- **Tip:** Incorporate different exercises and routines to avoid monotony. Experimenting with diverse exercises keeps the practice exciting and challenges the body.

Try New Challenges:
- **Tip:** Occasionally challenge yourself with new, slightly more advanced exercises. It stimulates growth and prevents plateauing.

4. Celebrate Milestones

Acknowledge Progress:
- **Tip:** Celebrate small victories along the way. Recognize and reward yourself for reaching milestones, reinforcing positive habits.

Track and Reflect:
- **Tip:** Regularly review progress through logs or journals. Reflecting on improvements provides motivation and highlights the journey's evolution.

5. Mind-Body Connection

Mindfulness Practice:

- **Tip:** Incorporate mindfulness into your sessions. Focus on the present moment, connecting breath with movement, enhancing the mind-body relationship.

Positive Self-Talk:

- **Tip:** Cultivate a positive inner dialogue. Encourage yourself, acknowledge efforts, and be kind when facing challenges.

Staying motivated in Wall Pilates involves understanding personal motivations, fostering a supportive environment, diversifying practice, celebrating achievements, and nurturing the mind-body connection. By applying these motivational tips, beginners can sustain enthusiasm, commitment, and joy in their Pilates journey.

28 DAY WALL PILATES EXERCISE PLAN

Week 1

Day 1: Core Strengthening	• Wall Crunches – 3 sets of 15 reps • Wall Plank Variations – Hold each variation for 30 seconds (Regular plank, side plank, forearm plank) • Wall Russian Twists – 3 sets of 12 reps (each side) • Wall Bridge – Hold for 30 seconds, 3 sets • Wall Knee Tucks – 3 sets of 12 reps
Day 2: Upper Body Toning	• Wall Push-Ups – 3 sets of 12 reps • Wall Chest Press – 3 sets of 12 reps • Wall Bicep Curls – 3 sets of 12 reps • Wall Tricep Dips – 3 sets of 12 reps • Wall Shoulder Taps – 3 sets of 10 taps (each shoulder)
Day 3: Lower Body Conditioning	• Wall Squats – 3 sets of 15 reps • Wall Lunges – 3 sets of 12 reps (each leg) • Wall Leg Press – 3 sets of 12 reps • Wall Calf Raises – 3 sets of 15 reps • Wall Hamstring Curls – 3 sets of 12 reps
Day 4: Balance and Stability	• Wall Balancing Pose – Hold for 45 seconds, 3 sets • Wall One-Legged Squat – 3 sets of 10 reps (each leg) • Wall Plank with Alternating Leg Lifts – 3 sets of 10 reps (each leg) • Wall Standing Hip Circles – 3 sets of 10 circles (clockwise and counterclockwise) • Wall Lateral Leg Swing – 3 sets of 10 swings (each leg)
Day 5: Flexibility and Stretching	• Wall Chest Opener Stretch – Hold for 30 seconds, 3 sets • Wall Spinal Twist Stretch – Hold for 30 seconds (each side), 3 sets • Wall Hamstring Stretch – Hold for 30 seconds (each leg), 3 sets • Wall Quadriceps Stretch – Hold for 30 seconds (each leg), 3 sets • Wall Glute Stretch – Hold for 30 seconds (each side), 3 sets
Day 6: Whole Body Integration	• Wall Roll Down – 3 sets of 10 reps • Wall Cat-Cow Stretch – 3 sets of 10 reps • Wall Full-Body Circles – 3 sets of 5 circles (clockwise and counterclockwise) • Wall Pelvic Tilts – 3 sets of 12 reps • Wall Side Bend – 3 sets of 12 reps (each side)
Day 7: Rest and Recovery	

Week 2

Day 1: Core Strengthening	• Wall Knee Extensions – 3 sets of 12 reps • Wall Plank with Arm Reach – 3 sets of 10 reps (each arm) • Wall Hamstring Curls – 3 sets of 12 reps • Wall Heel Raises for Balance – 3 sets of 15 reps • Wall Upper Back Stretch – Hold for 30 seconds, 3 sets
Day 2: Upper Body Toning	• Wall Side Crunches – 3 sets of 15 reps (each side) • Wall Tricep Stretch – Hold for 30 seconds (each arm), 3 sets • Wall Hip Hinge – 3 sets of 12 reps • Wall Standing Twist – 3 sets of 12 reps (each side) • Wall Toe Taps for Stability – 3 sets of 15 reps (each foot)
Day 3: Lower Body Conditioning	• Wall Leg Raises – 3 sets of 12 reps (each leg) • Wall Shoulder Taps – 3 sets of 10 taps (each shoulder) • Wall Side Leg Lifts – 3 sets of 12 reps (each leg) • Wall Clock Arm Stretch – Hold for 30 seconds (each arm), 3 sets • Wall Quadriceps Stretch – Hold for 30 seconds (each leg), 3 sets
Day 4: Balance and Stability	• Wall Roll Down – 3 sets of 10 reps • Wall Chest Press – 3 sets of 12 reps • Wall Standing Hip Circles – 3 sets of 10 circles (clockwise and counterclockwise) • Wall Russian Twists – 3 sets of 12 reps (each side) • Wall Balancing Pose – Hold for 45 seconds, 3 sets
Day 5: Flexibility and Stretching	• Wall Plank Variations – Hold each variation for 30 seconds (Regular plank, side plank, forearm plank) • Wall Calf Raises – 3 sets of 15 reps • Wall Wrist Flexor Stretch – Hold for 30 seconds (each arm), 3 sets • Wall Hip Abduction – 3 sets of 12 reps (each leg) • Wall Bridge – Hold for 30 seconds, 3 sets
Day 6: Whole Body Integration	• Wall Push-Ups – 3 sets of 12 reps • Wall Leg Press – 3 sets of 12 reps • Wall Wrist Extensor Stretch – Hold for 30 seconds (each arm), 3 sets • Wall Lateral Leg Swing – 3 sets of 10 swings (each leg) • Wall Full-Body Circles – 3 sets of 5 circles (clockwise and counterclockwise)
Day 7: Rest and Recovery	

Week 3

Day 1: Core Strengthening	• Wall Knee Tucks – 3 sets of 12 reps • Wall Angels – 3 sets of 10 reps • Wall Hamstring Stretch – Hold for 30 seconds (each leg), 3 sets • Wall One-Legged Squat – 3 sets of 10 reps (each leg) • Wall Standing Twist – 3 sets of 12 reps (each side)
Day 2: Upper Body Toning	• Wall Side Leg Raises for Stability – 3 sets of 12 reps (each leg) • Wall Bicep Curls – 3 sets of 12 reps • Wall Hip Flexor Stretch – Hold for 30 seconds (each leg), 3 sets • Wall Chest Opener Stretch – Hold for 30 seconds, 3 sets • Wall Roll Down – 3 sets of 10 reps
Day 3: Lower Body Conditioning	• Wall Leg Press – 3 sets of 12 reps • Wall Tricep Dips – 3 sets of 12 reps • Wall Glute Stretch – Hold for 30 seconds (each side), 3 sets • Wall Plank with Alternating Leg Lifts – 3 sets of 10 reps (each leg) • Wall Pelvic Tilts – 3 sets of 12 reps
Day 4: Balance and Stability	• Wall Crunches – 3 sets of 15 reps • Wall Push-Ups – 3 sets of 12 reps • Wall Quadriceps Stretch – Hold for 30 seconds (each leg), 3 sets • Wall Cat-Cow Stretch – 3 sets of 10 reps • Wall Calf Raises – 3 sets of 15 reps
Day 5: Flexibility and Stretching	• Wall Lunges – 3 sets of 12 reps (each leg) • Wall Plank with Arm Reach – 3 sets of 10 reps (each arm) • Wall Full-Body Circles – 3 sets of 5 circles (clockwise and counterclockwise) • Wall Side Bend – 3 sets of 12 reps (each side) • Wall Balancing Pose – Hold for 45 seconds, 3 sets
Day 6: Whole Body Integration	• Wall Russian Twists – 3 sets of 12 reps (each side) • Wall Shoulder Taps – 3 sets of 10 taps (each shoulder) • Wall Wrist Flexor Stretch – Hold for 30 seconds (each arm), 3 sets • Wall Hamstring Curls – 3 sets of 12 reps • Wall Heel Raises for Balance – 3 sets of 15 reps
Day 7: Rest and Recovery	

Week 4

Day 1: **Core Strengthening**	• Wall Russian Twists – 3 sets of 12 reps (each side) • Wall Plank Variations – Hold each variation for 30 seconds (Regular plank, side plank, forearm plank) • Wall Knee Tucks – 3 sets of 12 reps • Wall Bridge – Hold for 30 seconds, 3 sets • Wall Leg Raises – 3 sets of 12 reps (each leg)
Day 2: **Upper Body Toning**	• Wall Chest Press – 3 sets of 12 reps • Wall Bicep Curls – 3 sets of 12 reps • Wall Shoulder Taps – 3 sets of 10 taps (each shoulder) • Wall Tricep Dips – 3 sets of 12 reps • Wall Wrist Extensor Stretch – Hold for 30 seconds (each arm), 3 sets
Day 3: **Lower Body Conditioning**	• Wall Squats – 3 sets of 15 reps • Wall Lunges – 3 sets of 12 reps (each leg) • Wall Calf Raises – 3 sets of 15 reps • Wall Hip Hinge – 3 sets of 12 reps • Wall Knee Extensions – 3 sets of 12 reps
Day 4: **Balance and Stability**	• Wall Balancing Pose – Hold for 45 seconds, 3 sets • Wall One-Legged Squat – 3 sets of 10 reps (each leg) • Wall Plank with Alternating Leg Lifts – 3 sets of 10 reps (each leg) • Wall Standing Hip Circles – 3 sets of 10 circles (clockwise and counterclockwise) • Wall Lateral Leg Swing – 3 sets of 10 swings (each leg)
Day 5: **Flexibility and Stretching**	• Wall Hamstring Stretch – Hold for 30 seconds (each leg), 3 sets • Wall Chest Opener Stretch – Hold for 30 seconds, 3 sets • Wall Quadriceps Stretch – Hold for 30 seconds (each leg), 3 sets • Wall Spinal Twist Stretch – Hold for 30 seconds (each side), 3 sets • Wall Glute Stretch – Hold for 30 seconds (each side), 3 sets
Day 6: **Whole Body Integration**	• Wall Roll Down – 3 sets of 10 reps • Wall Cat-Cow Stretch – 3 sets of 10 reps • Wall Pelvic Tilts – 3 sets of 12 reps • Wall Full-Body Circles – 3 sets of 5 circles (clockwise and counterclockwise) • Wall Side Bend – 3 sets of 12 reps (each side)
Day 7: **Rest and Recovery**	Remember to listen to your body and modify exercises as needed. It's essential to maintain proper form throughout each exercise to prevent injury and maximize effectiveness. Additionally, stay hydrated and fuel your body with nutritious foods to support your workouts. Enjoy your weeks of wall Pilates!

15—MINUTE MORNING WALL PILATES ROUTINES

Starting your day with a 15-minute Wall Pilates routine can invigorate your body and mind, setting a positive tone for the day ahead. These routines are designed to gently awaken muscles, enhance flexibility, and promote mindfulness.

Morning Routine 1: Energizing Wake-Up Flow

1. Standing Wall Roll-Down
- **Muscles Engaged:** Hamstrings, Spine
- **Execution:** Stand with your back against the wall, feet hip-width apart. Slowly roll your spine down, reaching towards the floor. Roll back up to standing, stacking each vertebra.

2. Wall Push-Ups
- **Muscles Engaged:** Chest, Shoulders, Triceps
- **Execution:** Stand facing the wall, arms extended. Perform push-ups against the wall, focusing on controlled movement and engaging the chest muscles.

3. Wall Squats
- **Muscles Engaged:** Quads, Glutes
- **Execution:** Lean against the wall, feet hip-width apart. Slide down until thighs are parallel to the floor, ensuring knees align with ankles. Return to standing.

4. Wall Sit and Arm Raises
- **Muscles Engaged:** Quads, Shoulders
- **Execution:** Lower into a seated position against the wall (as if sitting in an invisible chair). While holding, raise arms overhead and lower back down.

5. Standing Wall Stretch
- **Muscles Engaged:** Hamstrings, Back
- **Execution:** Extend one leg forward, heel against the wall. Lean forward, feeling a gentle stretch in the hamstring. Repeat with the other leg.

Morning Routine 2: Core Strengthening Awakening

1. Wall Knee Tucks
- **Muscles Engaged:** Core, Hip Flexors
- **Execution:** Start in a plank position with hands on the floor, feet against the wall. Bring knees towards the chest, engaging the core. Return to plank position.

2. Wall Crunches
- **Muscles Engaged:** Abdominals
- **Execution:** Lie on your back, feet against the wall, knees bent. Perform crunches, lifting your upper body towards your knees.

3. Wall Side Plank
- **Muscles Engaged:** Obliques, Core
- **Execution:** Lie on your side, supporting your body on the forearm against the wall. Lift your hips off the ground, forming a straight line. Hold and switch sides.

4. Wall Leg Raises
- **Muscles Engaged:** Lower Abs, Hip Flexors
- **Execution:** Lie on your back, legs extended up the wall. Lower legs towards the floor, engaging lower abs, then return to the starting position.

5. Wall Cobra Stretch
- **Muscles Engaged:** Back, Chest
- **Execution:** Lie facing the wall, palms on the floor. Push up, arching the back gently while keeping hips grounded for a back stretch.

Morning Routine 3: Dynamic Mobility Start

1. Wall Arm Circles
- **Muscles Engaged:** Shoulders, Arms
- **Execution:** Stand facing the wall, arms extended. Make circular motions with arms against the wall, changing direction after a few rotations.

2. Wall Hamstring Stretch
- **Muscles Engaged:** Hamstrings
- **Execution:** Lie on your back, one leg extended up the wall, the other on the floor. Gently pull the extended leg towards you for a hamstring stretch.

3. Wall Bridge
- **Muscles Engaged:** Glutes, Hamstrings, Core
- **Execution:** Lie on your back, feet on the wall, knees bent. Lift your hips off the floor, forming a straight line from shoulders to knees.

4. Wall Shoulder Opener
- **Muscles Engaged:** Shoulders, Chest
- **Execution:** Stand facing the wall, arm at shoulder height. Rotate your body away from the wall, feeling a stretch in the chest and shoulders.

5. Wall Lunge Stretch
- **Muscles Engaged:** Quadriceps, Hip Flexors
- **Execution:** Lunge forward with one leg, placing the foot against the wall. Lean forward, feeling a stretch in the front of the thigh and hip.

Morning Routine 4: Balance and Stability Boost

1. Wall Balance Challenge
- **Muscles Engaged:** Core, Lower Body
- **Execution:** Stand on one leg, with the other foot resting on the wall. Hold the position, engaging core and leg muscles for balance.

2. Wall Side Leg Lifts
- **Muscles Engaged:** Outer Thighs, Glutes
- **Execution:** Lie on your side, legs extended, top leg against the wall. Lift the top leg, focusing on the outer thigh muscles.

3. Wall Plank with Leg Lift
- **Muscles Engaged:** Core, Shoulders, Glutes
- **Execution:** Begin in a plank position facing the wall. Lift one leg up behind you, engaging the glutes, and lower back down.

4. Wall Calf Raises
- **Muscles Engaged:** Calves
- **Execution:** Stand facing the wall, feet hip-width apart. Rise onto the balls of your feet, lifting heels off the floor.

5. Wall Hip Opener Stretch
- **Muscles Engaged:** Hips, Groin
- **Execution:** Lie on your back, knees bent. Place one ankle on the opposite knee, gently pressing the knee away from you for a hip stretch.

15—MINUTE EVENING WALL PILATES ROUTINES

These evening Wall Pilates routines offer diverse stretches and poses aimed at relaxation, flexibility, and restoration for beginners, promoting a peaceful end to the day.

Evening Routine 1: Relaxation and Release

1. Wall Chest Opener
- **Muscles Engaged:** Chest, Shoulders
- **Execution:** Stand facing the wall, arm at shoulder height. Rotate your body away from the wall, feeling a stretch in the chest and shoulders.

2. Wall Seated Twist
- **Muscles Engaged:** Obliques, Spine
- **Execution:** Sit against the wall with legs extended. Twist your torso, placing one hand on the opposite knee, and gaze behind for a gentle spinal twist.

3. Wall Supported Forward Fold
- **Muscles Engaged:** Hamstrings, Lower Back
- **Execution:** Sit close to the wall, extend legs up the wall, hinge at the hips, and fold forward. Allow gravity to deepen the stretch.

4. Wall Relaxation Pose
- **Muscles Engaged:** Full Body Relaxation
- **Execution:** Lie on your back, legs resting up the wall, arms by your sides. Close your eyes, focusing on deep breathing and relaxation for a calming finish.

Evening Routine 2: Deep Stretch and Unwind

1. Wall Lunge Stretch
- **Muscles Engaged:** Quadriceps, Hip Flexors
- **Execution:** Lunge forward with one leg, placing the foot against the wall. Lean forward, feeling a stretch in the front of the thigh and hip.

2. Wall Child's Pose
- **Muscles Engaged:** Lower Back, Hips
- **Execution:** Kneel facing the wall, hips resting against the wall, arms extended. Relax into a comfortable Child's Pose against the wall.

3. Wall Figure-4 Stretch

- **Muscles Engaged:** Glutes, Hips
- **Execution:** Lie close to the wall, one foot against the wall, cross the other ankle over the knee, gently pressing the knee away for a hip stretch.

4. Wall Reclining Twist

- **Muscles Engaged:** Spine, Torso
- **Execution:** Lie on your back, knees bent. Shift hips close to the wall, lower knees to one side, keeping shoulders grounded for a gentle spinal twist.

Evening Routine 3: Serene Balance and Stability

1. Wall Supported Tree Pose

- **Muscles Engaged:** Legs, Balance
- **Execution:** Stand near the wall, place one foot on the inner thigh, finding balance. Use the wall for support as needed.

2. Wall Seated Twist

- **Muscles Engaged:** Obliques, Spine
- **Execution:** Sit against the wall with legs extended. Twist your torso, placing one hand on the opposite knee, and gaze behind for a gentle spinal twist.

3. Wall Hip Flexor Stretch

- **Muscles Engaged:** Hip Flexors, Quadriceps
- **Execution:** Kneel facing away from the wall, one foot against the wall, gently leaning forward to feel a stretch in the hip flexors.

4. Wall Supported Forward Bend

- **Muscles Engaged:** Hamstrings, Spine
- **Execution:** Sit close to the wall, extend legs up the wall, hinge at the hips, and fold forward. Use the wall for support as you deepen the stretch.

Evening Routine 4: Calm and Restorative Flow

1. Wall Supported Butterfly Stretch

- **Muscles Engaged:** Inner Thighs, Groin
- **Execution:** Sit close to the wall, soles of the feet together, knees falling outward. Allow gravity to assist in opening the hips.

2. Wall Supported Supine Twist

- **Muscles Engaged:** Spine, Chest
- **Execution:** Lie on your back, knees bent, feet against the wall. Lower knees to one side, keeping shoulders grounded for a gentle spinal twist.

3. Wall Supported Legs-Up-The-Wall Pose

- **Muscles Engaged:** Lower Body Relaxation
- **Execution:** Lie on your back, extending legs up the wall. Relax into the pose, focusing on deep breathing and relaxation.

4. Wall Savasana

- **Muscles Engaged:** Full Body Relaxation
- **Execution:** Lie flat on your back, arms by your sides, palms facing up. Close your eyes and relax every muscle, focusing on deep, rhythmic breathing.

CONCLUSION

The journey through Wall Pilates for beginners has been a transformative experience. It fosters growth in physical strength, mental resilience, and overall well-being. Each chapter has laid the foundation for a fulfilling and sustainable practice, guiding beginners towards a holistic approach to health and fitness.

Reflecting on the Pilates Routine

Through this guide, beginners have explored the fundamental principles, techniques, and diverse exercises unique to Wall Pilates. It has been a journey of self-discovery, a journey to understand the nuances of movement, breath, and the crucial connection between mind and body.

Nurturing Mind-Body Harmony

The practice of Wall Pilates extends beyond mere physical exercise; it cultivates a deep connection between the mind and body. The emphasis on breath, mindfulness, and precise movements has heightened awareness of the body's capabilities and limitations.

Fostering Growth and Adaptability

The chapters on progress tracking, setting goals, and embracing adaptability have instilled a mindset of continual improvement. Embracing challenges as opportunities for growth and staying adaptable to evolving needs or physical changes are pivotal in sustaining progress.

Empowering Wellness Beyond Exercises

Beyond the physical aspects, Wall Pilates has empowered beginners to create a nurturing environment for holistic wellness. It emphasizes the movements against the wall and the importance of community, a positive mindset, and embracing diverse strategies for motivation and resilience.

A Journey, Not a Destination

As beginners conclude this guide, it's essential to remember that the Pilates journey is ongoing. It's about progress, not perfection; about consistency, not occasional intensity. Each step taken, each mindful breath, and each exercise practiced contributes to a healthier, more vibrant lifestyle.

Final Words

In concluding this book, remember that the principles learned here are not confined to the pages but are meant to be integrated into daily life. Embrace the joy, the challenges, and the rewards of the Pilates journey, staying committed to personal growth, well-being, and the lifelong pursuit of a healthier self.

WEEKLY FITNESS MONITORING

MONDAY

Meals	WATER
B:	
L:	
S:	
D:	
Workout:	Calories in:
Cardio _____	
Strength _____	Calories out:

TUESDAY

Meals	WATER
B:	
L:	
S:	
D:	
Workout:	Calories in:
Cardio _____	
Strength _____	Calories out:

WEEKLY
FITNESS MONITORING
Sheet

Month: _____

Week: _____

WEDNESDAY

Meals	WATER
B:	
L:	
S:	
D:	
Workout:	Calories in:
Cardio _____	
Strength _____	Calories out:

THUESDAY

Meals	WATER
B:	
L:	
S:	
D:	
Workout:	Calories in:
Cardio _____	
Strength _____	Calories out:

SUNDAY

Meals	WATER
B:	
L:	
S:	
D:	
Workout:	Calories in:
Cardio _____	
Strength _____	Calories out:

FRIDAY

Meals	WATER
B:	
L:	
S:	
D:	
Workout:	Calories in:
Cardio _____	
Strength _____	Calories out:

SATURDAY

Meals	WATER
B:	
L:	
S:	
D:	
Workout:	Calories in:
Cardio _____	
Strength _____	Calories out:

NOTES

_____

_____

_____

_____

_____

_____

For your convenience, a PDF file with a fitness tracker is provided via a link with bonuses for easy printing and placement wherever desired.

PAUSE! BEFORE YOU PROCEED

Greetings, fellow Pilates enthusiasts,

Within the pages of this Wall Pilates guide, I trust you've discovered a wellspring of rejuvenation, strength, and empowerment. Each exercise is not just a movement but a pathway to inner balance and vitality, tailored with precision to harness the transformative power of the wall pilates.

Every stretch, posture, and tip shared in this book reflects my commitment to your holistic health and fulfillment.

Your feedback, dear reader, is not merely appreciated; it's essential. Each comment serves as a cornerstone upon which I refine my craft, ensuring that future editions of this book resonate even more deeply with your needs and aspirations. This dialogue we share transcends the boundaries of the printed page; it's a connection that fosters growth and mutual support.

As a gesture of gratitude for welcoming this guide into your life, I've curated an exclusive bonus available through the link below. Consider it a token of appreciation for embarking on this journey of self-discovery and transformation with me.

ACCESS YOUR SPECIAL BONUS HERE!

https://wallpilates.site/

If you have any questions, suggestions, or feedback, please don't hesitate to reach out to us via email sophy.harrington@proton.me.

We greatly value your input and are always open to hearing from you. Rest assured, every word you share will be treasured and pondered upon.

With boundless gratitude and anticipation,

Sophy Harrington